Crystallization-Study
of the
**Epistles
of John**

Volume One

Witness Lee

The
Holy
Word
for
Morning
Revival

Living Stream Ministry
Anaheim, CA • www.lsm.org

First Edition, July 2007.

ISBN 0-7363-3501-3

Published by

Living Stream Ministry
2431 W. La Palma Ave., Anaheim, CA 92801 U.S.A.
P. O. Box 2121, Anaheim, CA 92814 U.S.A.

Printed in the United States of America

07 08 09 10 11 / 6 5 4 3 2 1

Contents

Preface

1. This book is intended as an aid to believers in developing a daily time of morning revival with the Lord in His word. At the same time, it provides a limited review of the Summer Training held July 2-7, 2007, in Anaheim, California, on the "Crystallization-study of the Epistles of John." Through intimate contact with the Lord in His word, the believers can be constituted with life and truth and thereby equipped to prophesy in the meetings of the church unto the building up of the Body of Christ.

2. The entire content of this book is taken from the *Crystallization-study Outlines: The Epistles of John,* the text and footnotes of the Recovery Version of the Bible, selections from the writings of Witness Lee and Watchman Nee, and *Hymns,* all of which are published by Living Stream Ministry.

3. The book is divided into weeks. One training message is covered per week. Each week presents first the message outline, followed by six daily portions, a hymn, and then some space for writing. The training outline has been divided into days, corresponding to the six daily portions. Each daily portion covers certain points and begins with a section entitled "Morning Nourishment." This section contains selected verses and a short reading that can provide rich spiritual nourishment through intimate fellowship with the Lord. The "Morning Nourishment" is followed by a section entitled "Today's Reading," a longer portion of ministry related to the day's main points. Each day's portion concludes with a short list of references for further reading and some space for the saints to make notes concerning their spiritual inspiration, enlightenment, and enjoyment to serve as a reminder of what they have received of the Lord that day.

4. The space provided at the end of each week is for composing a short prophecy. This prophecy can be composed by considering all of our daily notes, the "harvest" of our inspirations during the week, and preparing a main

point with some sub-points to be spoken in the church meetings for the organic building up of the Body of Christ.

5. Following the last week in this volume, we have provided reading schedules for both the Old and New Testaments in the Recovery Version with footnotes. These schedules are arranged so that one can read through both the Old and New Testaments of the Recovery Version with footnotes in two years.

6. As a practical aid to the saints' feeding on the Word throughout the day, we have provided verse cards at the end of the volume, which correspond to each day's scripture reading. These may be cut out and carried along as a source of spiritual enlightenment and nourishment in the saints' daily lives.

7. The *Crystallization-study Outlines* were compiled by Living Stream Ministry from the writings of Witness Lee and Watchman Nee. The outlines, footnotes, and references in the Recovery Version of the Bible are by Witness Lee. All of the other references cited in this publication are from the published ministry of Witness Lee and Watchman Nee.

Summer Training

(July 2-7, 2007)

CRYSTALLIZATION-STUDY OF THE EPISTLES OF JOHN

Banners:

The fellowship of the eternal life,
the flow of the eternal life within all the believers,
is the reality of living in the Body of Christ.

We know the Triune God
by experiencing and enjoying Him
as the One who dwells in our spirit and
desires to spread into our heart.

By the anointing of the all-inclusive compound Spirit,
who is the composition of the Divine Trinity,
we know and enjoy the Father, the Son, and
the Spirit as our life and life supply.

The Son of God has given us an understanding
so that we might know the true One,
the genuine and real God,
and be one with Him organically
in His Son Jesus Christ, who is eternal life to us.

The Fellowship of the Eternal Life— the Reality of Living in the Body of Christ

Scripture Reading: 1 John 1:1—2:2

Day 1   **I. John's Epistles (especially his first Epistle) unfold the mystery of the fellowship of the eternal life (1 John 1:3-4, 6-7):**

A. Fellowship is the flow of the eternal life within all the believers, illustrated by the flow of the water of life in the New Jerusalem; the reality of the Body of Christ, the church life in actuality, is the flow of the Lord Jesus within us, and this flowing One must have the preeminence within us (vv. 2-4; Rev. 22:1; Col. 1:18b; cf. Ezek. 47:1).

B. Fellowship is the flowing Triune God—the Father is the fountain of life, the Son is the spring of life, and the Spirit is the river of life; this flowing issues in the totality of eternal life—the New Jerusalem (John 4:14b; Rev. 22:1-2).

C. Fellowship is the imparting of the Triune God— the Father, the Son, and the Spirit—into the believers as their unique portion and blessing for them to enjoy today and for eternity (1 Cor. 1:9; 2 Cor. 13:14; Num. 6:22-27).

D. Fellowship indicates a putting away of private interests and a joining with others for a certain common purpose; hence, to be in the divine fellowship is to put aside our private interests and join with the apostles and the Triune God for the carrying out of God's purpose (Acts 2:42; 1 John 1:3).

Day 2   E. Fellowship comes from teaching; if we teach wrongly and differently from the apostles' teaching, the teaching of God's economy, our teaching will produce a sectarian, divisive fellowship (Acts 2:42; 1 Tim. 1:3-6; 6:3-4; 2 Cor. 3:8-9; 5:18).

F. First John reveals the principles of the divine fellowship, 2 John reveals that we must have no fellowship with those who deny Christ (vv. 7-11), and 3 John reveals that we should stay in the one fellowship of God's family by sending forward those who travel for the gospel and the ministry of the word in a manner worthy of God and by not loving to be first in the church (vv. 5-10).

Day 3 II. **The fellowship of the eternal life is the reality of living in the Body of Christ in the oneness of the Spirit (1 Cor. 10:16-18; Acts 2:42; Eph. 4:3):**

A. We enter into the vertical aspect of the divine fellowship by the divine Spirit, the Holy Spirit; this aspect of fellowship refers to our fellowship with the Triune God in our loving Him (2 Cor. 13:14; 1 John 1:3, 6; Mark 12:30).

B. We enter into the horizontal aspect of the divine fellowship by the human spirit; this aspect of fellowship refers to our fellowship with one another by the exercise of our spirit in our loving one another (Phil. 2:1; Rev. 1:10; 1 John 1:2-3, 7; 1 Cor. 16:18; Mark 12:31; Rom. 13:8-10; Gal. 5:13-15).

C. The one divine fellowship is an interwoven fellowship—the horizontal fellowship is interwoven with the vertical fellowship:

1. The initial experience of the apostles was the vertical fellowship with the Father and with His Son Jesus Christ, but when the apostles reported the eternal life to others, they experienced the horizontal aspect of the divine fellowship (1 John 1:2-3; cf. Acts 2:42).

2. Our horizontal fellowship with the saints brings us into vertical fellowship with the Lord; then our vertical fellowship with the Lord brings us into horizontal fellowship with the saints.

3. We must maintain both the vertical and horizontal aspects of the divine fellowship in order to be healthy spiritually (cf. 1 John 1:7, 9).

D. The divine fellowship is everything in the Christian life:
  1. When fellowship disappears, God also disappears; God comes as the fellowship (2 Cor. 13:14; Rev. 22:1).
  2. In this divine fellowship God is interwoven with us; this interweaving is the mingling of God and man to bring the divine constituent into our spiritual being for our growth and transformation in life (Lev. 2:4-5).
  3. The divine fellowship blends us, tempers us, adjusts us, harmonizes us, and mingles us together into one Body (1 Cor. 10:16-18; 12:24-25).

Day 4 III. **In order to remain in the enjoyment of the divine fellowship, we need to take Christ as our sin offering for the indwelling sin in our nature and as our trespass offering for the sinful deeds in our conduct (1 John 1:8-9; 3:20-21; Lev. 4:3; 5:6; John 1:29; Rom. 8:3; 2 Cor. 5:21; 1 Pet. 2:24-25):**
  A. Sin is the evil nature of Satan, who injected himself into man through Adam's fall and has now become the sinful nature of lawlessness that is dwelling, acting, and working as a law in fallen man (Rom. 5:12, 19a, 21a; 6:14; 7:11, 14, 17-23; Psa. 51:5; 1 John 3:4; cf. 2 Thes. 2:3, 7-8).
  B. Taking Christ as our sin offering means that our old man is dealt with (Rom. 6:6), that sin in the nature of fallen man is condemned (8:3), that Satan as sin itself is destroyed (Heb. 2:14), that the world is judged, and that the ruler of the world is cast out (John 12:31):
    1. The word *ruler* in "the ruler of this world" implies authority or power and the struggle for power (Luke 4:5-8; cf. Matt. 20:20-21, 24; 3 John 9).
    2. The struggle for power is the result, the issue, of the flesh, sin, Satan, the world,

and the ruler of the world (Gal. 5:16-17, 24-26).

3. The law of sin in our flesh is the spontaneous power, strength, and energy to struggle with God; the law of the sin offering is the law of the life of the pneumatic Christ, whom we enjoy, to automatically and spontaneously free us from the law of sin (Rom. 7:23; 8:2; Lev. 6:24-30; cf. 7:1-10).

C. We partake of Christ as our sin offering in the sense of enjoying Him as our life, the life that bears others' sins, so that we may be able to bear the problems of God's people by ministering Christ to them as the sin-dealing life for them to be kept in the oneness of the Spirit (1 John 5:16; Lev. 10:17).

Day 5

D. Through our genuine, intimate, living, and loving fellowship with God, who is light (1 John 1:5; Col. 1:12), we will realize that we are sinful, and we will take Christ as our sin offering and trespass offering:

1. The more we love the Lord and enjoy Him, the more we will know how evil we are (Isa. 6:5; Luke 5:8; Rom. 7:18).

2. Realizing that we have a sinful nature and taking Christ as our sin offering cause us to be judged and subdued, and this realization preserves us, for it causes us not to have any confidence in ourselves (Phil. 3:3; cf. Exo. 4:6).

3. Man, created by God for the purpose of expressing and representing God, should be for nothing other than God and should be absolutely for God; thus, anything we do out of ourselves, whether good or evil, is for ourselves, and since it is for ourselves and not for God, it is sinful in the eyes of God; sin is being for the self (Gen. 1:26; Isa. 43:7; Rom. 3:23):

  a. Serving the Lord for ourselves is sin; preaching ourselves is sin (Num. 28:2; 2 Kings 5:20-27; Matt. 7:22-23; 2 Cor. 4:5).
  b. Doing our righteous deeds, such as giving alms, praying, and fasting, for ourselves to express and display ourselves is sin (Matt. 6:1-6).
  c. Loving others for ourselves (for our name, position, benefit, and pride) is sin; raising up our children for ourselves and for our future is sin (Luke 14:12-14; cf. 1 Cor. 7:14).

4. The Lord uses our failures to show us how horrible, ugly, and abominable we are, causing us to forsake all that is from the self and to completely depend on God (Psa. 51; Luke 22:31-32; Rom. 8:28).

Day 6   E. To take Christ as the reality of the trespass offering is to experience Him as the redeeming One, the shining One, and the reigning One in order to enjoy Him as the supply of life in the fellowship of life (1 John 1:1—2:2; Rev. 21:21, 23; 22:1-2):

1. In taking Christ as our trespass offering, we need to make a thorough confession of all our sins and impurity to have a good and pure conscience (Acts 24:16; 1 Tim. 1:5, 19; 3:9; 2 Tim. 1:3; Heb. 9:14; 10:22).
2. If we confess our sins, God is faithful in His word to forgive us our sins and righteous in His redemption to cleanse us from all unrighteousness; furthermore, Christ as our elder Brother is our Advocate with the Father to restore our interrupted fellowship with the Father that we may abide in the enjoyment of the divine fellowship (1 John 1:7, 9; 2:1-2).
3. The cleansing of the blood of Jesus the Son of God solves the problem of separation

from God, the problem of guilt in our conscience, and the problem of accusations
from Satan, thus enabling us to have a daily
life full of God's presence (Psa. 103:1-4,
12-13; 32:1-2; Rev. 12:10-11).

4. Taking Christ as our trespass offering with
the confession of our sins in the divine light
is the way to drink Christ as the living
water for us to become the New Jerusalem
(John 4:14-18).

5. Taking Christ as our trespass offering to
receive the forgiveness of sins issues in our
fearing God and loving God (Psa. 130:4;
Luke 7:47-50).

IV. As we are enjoying Christ in the divine
fellowship, we continually experience a
cycle in our spiritual life of four crucial
things—the eternal life, the fellowship of
the eternal life, the divine light, and the
blood of Jesus the Son of God; such a cycle
brings us onward in the growth of the
divine life until we reach the maturity of
life to corporately arrive at a full-grown
man, at the measure of the stature of the
fullness of Christ (1 John 1:1-9; Heb. 6:1;
Eph. 4:13).

Morning Nourishment

1 John   That which we have seen and heard we report also
1:3   to you that you also may have fellowship with us,
         and indeed our fellowship is with the Father and
         with His Son Jesus Christ.
Rev.   And he showed me a river of water of life, bright as
22:1   crystal, proceeding out of the throne of God and of
         the Lamb in the middle of its street.
2 Cor.   The grace of the Lord Jesus Christ and the love of
13:14   God and the fellowship of the Holy Spirit be with
         you all.

The Greek word for fellowship, *koinonia,* means joint participation, common participation. It is the issue of the eternal life and is actually the flow of the eternal life within all the believers, who have received and possess the divine life. It is illustrated by the flow of the water of life in the New Jerusalem (Rev. 22:1). Hence, all genuine believers are in this fellowship (Acts 2:42). It is carried on by the Spirit in our regenerated spirit. Hence, it is called "the fellowship of the Holy Spirit" (2 Cor. 13:14) and "fellowship of [our] spirit" (Phil. 2:1). It is in this fellowship of the eternal life that we the believers participate in all the Father and the Son are and have done for us; that is, we enjoy the love of the Father and the grace of the Son by virtue of the fellowship of the Spirit. Such a fellowship was first the apostles' portion in enjoying the Father and the Son through the Spirit. Hence, it is called "the fellowship of the apostles" (Acts 2:42) and "our [the apostles'] fellowship" in 1 John 1:3, a fellowship with the Father and with His Son Jesus Christ. It is a divine mystery. This mysterious fellowship of the eternal life should be considered the subject of this Epistle. (*Life-study of 1 John,* p. 42)

Today's Reading

Fellowship is a common participation, a joint participation. Therefore, to have fellowship is to have a corporate participation in something. The fellowship of the divine life is the issue and flow of the divine life. Because the divine life is organic, rich, moving, and active, it has a particular issue, a certain kind of outcome. The issue, the outcome, of the divine life is the fellowship of life....The fellowship of the divine life flows out of God and through His people in order to reach every part of the Body of Christ, which will consummate in the New Jerusalem.

The fellowship of the divine life, or the flow of the divine life, is the fellowship of the Spirit. Second Corinthians 13:14 says, "The grace of the Lord Jesus Christ and the love of God and the fellowship of the Holy Spirit be with you all." Here we see that the love of God is the source, that the grace of Christ is the course, and that the fellowship of the Spirit is the flow of the course. It is this flow that brings the grace of Christ and the love of God to us for our enjoyment. Therefore, the fellowship of the divine life is called the fellowship of the Holy Spirit. (*Life-study of 1 John,* pp. 42-43)

[In Ezekiel 47:1] the waters come from the right side of the house. In the Bible, the right side is the highest position, the first place. Thus, the flow of life must have the preeminence, the first place. This tells us that we should never forget, neglect, or miss the flow of living water, the flow of life. We have to check with ourselves all the time: "Do we have the flow within us? Are we in the flow?" If we are in the flow, everything is all right regardless of the situation that we are in. As long as we are in the flow, we are one with the Lord. We have to pay our full attention to the flow and pay the price to get ourselves into the flow. This flow must be on the right side; it must be in the first place; it must have the preeminence. (*The Crucial Revelation of Life in the Scriptures,* pp. 52-53)

Further Reading: Life-study of 1 John, msg. 5; *The Crucial Revelation of Life in the Scriptures,* ch. 5; *The Mending Ministry of John,* ch. 7; *The Seven Mysteries in the First Epistle of John,* ch. 2

Enlightenment and inspiration: _____

_____

_____

_____

Morning Nourishment

Acts   And they continued steadfastly in the teaching
2:42   and the fellowship of the apostles, in the breaking
       of bread and the prayers.

[In Acts 2:42] four items are divided into two groups. The teaching and the fellowship are related to the apostles, while the breaking of bread and the prayers are not related to the apostles. This means that a person who prays does not need to pray in something related to the apostles. If saints break bread, they do not need to break bread in something related to the apostles. But no one has the freedom in the divine economy to teach whatever he likes to teach. Our teaching must be restricted by the limit and by the sphere of the apostles' teaching. Furthermore, a fellowship outside the fellowship of the apostles is divisive. Our fellowship must be inside the fellowship of the apostles. The apostles' teaching is unique, and the apostles' fellowship is also unique. (*The God-ordained Way to Practice the New Testament Economy*, p. 149)

Today's Reading

The apostles' teaching is the teaching concerning Christ's person and redemptive work (2 John 9-11). It is also the teaching concerning God's economy in faith (1 Tim. 1:3-4). God's economy is not to have a mission field for preaching the gospel or to have a Bible school to teach the truths. God's economy is to dispense or impart the Triune God into His chosen and redeemed people to be their life and everything that they might be regenerated and transformed into the proper material for the building up of the Body of Christ that God may have a corporate expression on the earth in many localities in this age with a view to the building up of the coming New Jerusalem for His eternal expression. If we limit ourselves to the apostles' teaching, the teaching concerning God's economy, we will be kept in oneness and will have one way for one goal. We must have a clear vision concerning God's economy; then we will never be misled. We will keep ourselves going toward the unique goal in the unique way.

Fellowship comes from the teaching. There should be only one unique teaching—the teaching of the apostles. Furthermore, there should be one unique fellowship which is produced by the apostles' teaching. What we teach will produce a kind of fellowship. If we teach wrongly and differently from the apostles' teaching, our teaching will produce a sectarian, divisive fellowship. If I teach baptism by immersion as a condition or a term for receiving the saints, this teaching will produce a Baptist fellowship.... Wrong teaching produces wrong, divisive fellowship. We can have one way for one goal by keeping ourselves strictly in the limit of the apostles' teaching and the apostles' fellowship. There should not be another fellowship besides the apostles' fellowship.

The apostles' fellowship is with the Father and the Son (1 John 1:3) and is also the fellowship of the Spirit (2 Cor. 13:14), which the apostles participated in and ministered to the believers through the preaching of the divine life (1 John 1:2-3). Preaching produces fellowship, and fellowship must be of the divine life. The blood circulation in our physical body...is the fellowship of our physical life. If this fellowship is stopped, disease or death can result. Cancer cells are cells that are outside the "fellowship of the physical body."...If we are going to keep the proper fellowship, we must learn to live by the divine life. When we live by the divine life, we are in the circulation of the divine life, the fellowship.

The apostles' fellowship is the fellowship in which the believers enjoy the divine life and through which they fellowship with one another in the spirit (Phil. 2:1; Acts 2:42)....This fellowship is altogether a matter of the divine life in the mingled spirit. We need to do everything in our spirit with the divine life. This unique fellowship is the genuine oneness of the Body of Christ as the unique ground for the believers to be kept one in Christ (Eph. 4:3-6). (*The God-ordained Way to Practice the New Testament Economy*, pp. 152-153, 155-157)

Further Reading: The God-ordained Way to Practice the New Testament Economy, ch. 17; A General Sketch of the New Testament in the Light of Christ and the Church, Part 3, ch. 31

Enlightenment and inspiration: _____

_____

_____

_____

Morning Nourishment

**Phil. If there is therefore any encouragement in Christ,
2:1 if any consolation of love, if any fellowship of spirit,
if any tenderheartedness and compassions.**

The divine fellowship has two aspects: the vertical aspect between God and us and the horizontal aspect among the believers. The horizontal aspect of the divine fellowship is by the human spirit. The vertical aspect of the divine fellowship is by the divine Spirit, the Holy Spirit (2 Cor. 13:14; 2 Tim. 4:22). The word *by* is actually not strong enough to express what we mean. The Spirit is not merely involved, wrapped up, or mingled with the fellowship. The Spirit Himself *is* the fellowship because the fellowship is the flow, the current, of the Spirit. This is like saying that the current of electricity is just the electricity itself. The current of electricity is electricity in motion. When the electricity stops, the current of electricity also stops. In the same way, the fellowship of the Holy Spirit mentioned in 2 Corinthians 13:14 is the Spirit moving….The divine fellowship is the Holy Spirit Himself. (*The Triune God to Be Life to the Tripartite Man*, pp. 149-150)

Today's Reading

We need to enter into the horizontal aspect of the divine fellowship by the human spirit (Phil. 2:1; Rev. 1:10)….To have real fellowship horizontally with one another, we need to exercise our spirit. If we exercise our spirit, we will never talk in a worldly manner or speak negatively about the saints or the churches;…the nature of our conversation will change because our spirit is holy (cf. 2 Cor. 6:6).

The two aspects of the divine fellowship require us to be in the two spirits, the Holy Spirit and the human spirit. These two spirits eventually become one (Rom. 8:16; 1 Cor. 6:17). When Paul charges us to walk according to spirit in Romans 8:4, he is speaking of the mingled spirit—the divine Spirit mingled with our human spirit. When we exercise our spirit to carry out the divine fellowship, we are fully sanctified, rescued, and saved from everything other than Christ. To be victorious, overcoming, sanctified, and transformed, we must exercise our spirit to carry out the two aspects of the divine fellowship.

The horizontal and vertical aspects of the divine fellowship are very closely related. We can see this from our experience. Sometimes, we may talk about other saints under the pretense of having fellowship about their situation, but our conversation is actually gossip. Afterwards, we often cannot pray, because our praying spirit is quenched by our gossip. But when we fellowship in a genuine way by exercising our spirit, we are eager to pray and contact the Lord. This shows how close the relationship is between the vertical and horizontal aspects of fellowship. The horizontal fellowship ushers us into the vertical fellowship. If two brothers exercise their spirit to have genuine, proper, horizontal fellowship, they will eventually be ushered into a very honest and sincere intercession. When they pray together, the two aspects of the divine fellowship are interwoven. The horizontal fellowship is interwoven with the vertical fellowship. This interwoven fellowship is the real fellowship.

Fellowship cannot have just one aspect alone. You cannot have the vertical fellowship without the horizontal fellowship. If you have a good time with the Lord in vertical fellowship, you will be eager to see the other saints in order to have fellowship with them. Once you have fellowship with the saints through prayer, you are brought into vertical fellowship with the Lord again. Your horizontal fellowship with the saints brings you into vertical fellowship with the Lord. Then your fellowship with the Lord brings you into horizontal fellowship with the saints. Thus, these two aspects are always interwoven, that is, they are always crisscrossing each other.

The divine fellowship is everything in the Christian life. The apostle Paul lived in this fellowship. When we live in the divine fellowship, our Christian life becomes very living, active, and full of impact. We need to fully enter into the experience of the divine fellowship in its two aspects by the two spirits. (*The Triune God to Be Life to the Tripartite Man,* pp. 152-153, 155)

Further Reading: The Triune God to Be Life to the Tripartite Man, msgs. 17-19; *The Divine and Mystical Realm,* ch. 6

Enlightenment and inspiration: _____

Morning Nourishment

**Lev.   ...If anyone sins without intent, in any of the things
4:2-3   which Jehovah has commanded not to be done, and
        does any one of them, if the anointed priest sins so
        as to bring guilt on the people, then let him present
        a bull of the herd without blemish to Jehovah for a
        sin offering for his sin that he committed.**

A number of times Leviticus 4 speaks of the sin of ignorance
(vv. 1-2, 13, 22, 27)....The sin of ignorance...signifies the sin in our
fallen nature, the indwelling sin....Many times we sin uninten-
tionally. These sins come from the indwelling sin. Sin came in
through Adam's fall and entered into the human race (Rom. 5:12).
Therefore, with all human beings there is something called sin.

In Romans 7 sin is personified, because it can dwell in us
(v. 17), kill us (v. 11), and do many things in us. Thus, sin is a living
person. We cannot find a verse which says that sin is Satan himself. However, the Bible indicates that sin is the nature of Satan.
Since sin is the nature of Satan, sin is actually Satan himself.
(*Life-study of Leviticus,* p. 171)

Today's Reading

Romans 7 is a picture of our experience not only before we
were saved but even today. Have you not discovered that there is
a war going on within you? On the one hand, we may say, "I love
the church." On the other hand, something within us says, "I do
not like the church."

Anything that is done out of our flesh is sin. In the eyes of God,
even our love that is out of the flesh is sin. Not only the bad things
are sin, but even the good things that are out of the flesh are sin. It
is the source, not the outcome or issue, that counts. This is the reason Galatians 5:24 says, "They who are of Christ Jesus have crucified the flesh with its passions and its lusts."

According to the human view, the flesh may seem to be good as
well as bad. But whether we are good, bad, or in the middle, as long
as we are flesh we are sin. The flesh is altogether one with sin (Rom.
8:3), and sin is altogether one with Satan. Actually, sin is Satan.

Furthermore, Satan is one with the world, and the world is one with the ruler of the world (John 12:31). These five things are one matter: the flesh, sin, Satan, the world, and the ruler of the world.

Today's world is related to the flesh, sin, Satan, and the ruler of the world. The word *ruler* here implies authority or power. The world is actually the struggle for power. Every person and every nation are struggling for power. Everywhere there is competition, rivalry, for power....This struggle for power is the result, the issue, of the flesh, sin, Satan, the world, and the ruler of the world.

The sin offering has a broad denotation. It deals not only with sin itself but also with our flesh, with Satan, the evil one in our flesh, with the world, and with the struggle for power.

We need to pray and take the Lord Jesus as our burnt offering, as the One who is absolute for God. Enjoying Christ as the burnt offering will lead us to take Him as our life supply, as our meal offering, which is Christ in His humanity becoming our daily food. We need to enjoy Him until we feel that we have peace with God, with ourselves, and with everyone. Immediately we will be in the light, and the light will shine within us, upon us, and around us. Then we will realize that we have sinned and that we are sin. This is the experience in 1 John chapter one. God is light (v. 5). In order to have fellowship with Him, we must walk in the light as He is in the light. If we do this, we will realize that we have something called sin (vv. 7-8).

We struggle with the Lord about many things. We love the Lord, we attend the church meetings, and we participate fully in the church life. On the surface everything appears to be fine. However, only we ourselves know how much we are in a struggle with God day after day. God wants us to be absolute for Him, but we may be willing to be absolute for Him only to a certain degree.... Instead of being utterly absolute for God, we engage in a power struggle with Him. (*Life-study of Leviticus,* pp. 172-174, 180-181)

Further Reading: Life-study of Leviticus, msgs. 18-19; *Life-study of 1 John,* msgs. 6-7

Enlightenment and inspiration: _____

_____

_____

_____

Morning Nourishment

**1 John But if we walk in the light as He is in the light, we
1:7   have fellowship with one another, and the blood of
       Jesus His Son cleanses us from every sin.**

When we believed in the Lord Jesus, we received Him as our
Redeemer....Receiving the Lord Jesus as our Redeemer includes
receiving Him as both the sin offering and the trespass offering.
Often we say that the blood of Jesus cleanses us....In 1 John 1:7
John speaks of the blood of Jesus that cleanses us from every sin.
This is the blood of the Lord Jesus as both the sin offering and the
trespass offering. (*Life-study of 1 John*, pp. 54-55)

Today's Reading

If we have never enjoyed Christ as the burnt offering, we cannot realize how sinful we are. We heard the gospel and repented,
realizing that we are sinful. But we cannot know how sinful we
are until we enjoy Christ as our burnt offering. The burnt offering
means that mankind, created by God for the purpose of expressing and representing Him, should be for nothing other than God
and should be absolutely for God. However, we are not absolutely
for God. We need to realize this and take Christ as our burnt offering. Only when we enjoy Christ as our burnt offering will we realize how sinful we are.

If we realize how sinful we are, we will know that our love as
well as our hate may be sinful....We may think that in the eyes of
God loving others is acceptable and hating others is not acceptable. But in the eyes of God we hate people for ourselves and also
love people for ourselves, not for God. From this point of view, loving others is just as sinful as hating others. Whatever we do for
ourselves and not for God—whether it is moral or immoral, good
or evil, a matter of love or of hate—is sinful in the eyes of God. As
long as you do a certain thing for yourself, it is sinful.

Neither our hatred nor our love is from our spirit. Rather, both
our hatred and our love are from our flesh, and both are from the
tree of the knowledge of good and evil. The tree of the knowledge
of good and evil signifies Satan. We should not think that only

doing evil is of Satan and doing good is not. Doing both good and evil may be of Satan. We need to realize that anything we do out of ourselves, whether good or evil, is for ourselves, and since it is for ourselves, it is sin.

I would point out once again that sin involves a power struggle. We may love others for ourselves—for our name, position, benefit, and pride....This kind of love is of Satan; it is in the flesh, and it is sin. Whatever is in the flesh is sin, whatever is sin in our flesh is Satan, and whatever is done there by Satan is the power struggle.

Because we may have hidden motives in doing spiritual things, the Lord Jesus spoke concerning those who do things apparently for God but actually for the purpose of advancing themselves...."Take care not to do your righteousness before men in order to be gazed at by them" (Matt. 6:1)...."Do not let your left hand know what your right hand is doing" (v. 3)...."When you pray, you shall not be like the hypocrites, because they love to pray standing in the synagogues and on the street corners, so that they may be seen by men" (v. 5)...."When you fast, do not be like the sullen-faced hypocrites, for they disfigure their faces so that they may appear to men to be fasting" (v. 16). Even in doing righteousness, giving alms, praying, and fasting there may be a power struggle with God. To do these things for ourselves and not for God is sinful in His eyes. Those who do such things for themselves give no ground to God; instead, all the ground is for themselves.

To take Christ as the sin offering is very deep. The experience of the sin offering is altogether related to our enjoyment of the Lord Jesus as our burnt offering. The more we love the Lord and enjoy Him, the more we will know how evil we are. Sometimes, when we love the Lord to the uttermost, we may feel that there is no place to hide ourselves. Paul had such a realization concerning himself. When he was seeking the Lord, he saw that there was nothing good in himself. (*Life-study of Leviticus,* pp. 184-186)

Further Reading: Life-study of Leviticus, msgs. 20, 25; *The Collected Works of Watchman Nee,* vol. 8, pp. 25-35

Enlightenment and inspiration: _____

_____

_____

_____

Morning Nourishment

1 John   ...If anyone sins, we have an Advocate with the
2:1-2   Father, Jesus Christ the Righteous; and He Him-
       self is the propitiation for our sins, and not for ours
       only but also for *those of* the whole world.

According to chapter one of [1 John], we have received the divine life, and we are enjoying it in the fellowship of life. In this fellowship we receive the divine light, and in this light we practice the truth. But we still need the warning concerning the sin that dwells in our flesh. We need to be careful and on the alert regarding indwelling sin.

Whenever we sin, we need to confess our sin to God. If we confess our sins, God is faithful in His word to forgive us our sins, and He is righteous in His redemption to cleanse us from all unrighteousness. This is wonderful. Nevertheless, as 2:1-2 indicates, we still need a Person, an Advocate with the Father, to take care of our case. Because we are not capable of handling the case ourselves, we need a heavenly attorney.

In chapter one John speaks of the blood of Jesus, and in chapter two, of our Advocate. Not only has God provided the blood of Jesus Christ, which was shed for us so that we may be forgiven and cleansed; God has also prepared Christ as our Advocate. First, the Lord Jesus shed His blood as the price of our redemption. Then after shedding His blood, He becomes our Advocate, our heavenly attorney, taking care of our case. How marvelous that our Advocate pays our debt and takes care of our case!

As the One who shed His blood for us, the Lord Jesus is the righteous One. He is right not only with the Father but also right with us. The Lord is our Paraclete (the anglicized form of *parakletos,* the Greek word rendered Advocate). He comes alongside to help us, He serves us, He takes care of us, and He provides whatever we need. We were in need of the cleansing blood; therefore, He provided us with His own blood for redemption and cleansing. We also need someone to take care of our case. Therefore, He is now our Advocate, our *parakletos.* (*Life-study of 1 John,* pp. 120-121)

Today's Reading

In [1 John] 1:1-7 we see a cycle in our spiritual life formed of four crucial things—the eternal life, the fellowship of the eternal life, the divine light, and the blood of Jesus the Son of God. Eternal life issues in the fellowship of the divine life, the fellowship of eternal life brings in the divine light, and the divine light increases the need of the blood of Jesus the Son of God so that we may have more eternal life. The more we have of eternal life, the more of its fellowship it brings to us. The more fellowship of the divine life we enjoy, the more divine light we receive. The more divine light we receive, the more we participate in the cleansing of the blood of Jesus. Such a cycle brings us onward in the growth of the divine life until we reach its maturity. (*Life-study of 1 John,* pp. 70-71)

By enjoying the Lord as the burnt offering and the meal offering, we realize that we are sinful. So we take Him as the sin offering and then as the trespass offering. This is what we see in chapter one of 1 John. As we are enjoying the Triune God in the divine fellowship, we realize that we still have sin inwardly and that we have committed sins outwardly. We then receive the cleansing of the precious blood. This becomes a cycle. The more we are cleansed, the more we enter into fellowship with the Triune God; the more we enjoy this fellowship, the more we are enlightened; and the more we are enlightened, the more we realize that we are sinful, even sin itself. It is by this cycle that we are delivered and saved from our self. Actually, we are delivered and saved from sin, from the flesh, from Satan, from the world, from the ruler of the world, and from the power struggle. The more we enjoy Christ, the less power struggle we will have with God. Eventually we will give every inch to Him. (*Life-study of Leviticus,* pp. 187-188)

Further Reading: Life-study of 1 John, msgs. 8, 13-14; *Life-study of Leviticus,* msgs. 21-22, 26; *The Collected Works of Witness Lee, 1963,* vol. 3, pp. 513-520

Enlightenment and inspiration: _____

_____
_____
_____

Hymns, #737

1   Life eternal brings us
       Fellowship of life,
    Fellowship in Spirit,
       Saving us from strife.

2   Life eternal gives us
       Fellowship divine;
    Thus the Lord as Spirit
       May with us combine.

3   It is life in Spirit
       Brings this fellowship;
    Fellowship in Spirit
       Doth with grace equip.

4   We, by life's enabling,
       Fellowship aright;
    Fellowship in Spirit
       Brings us into light.

5   By the outward cleansing,
       Fellowship we keep;
    Inwardly anointed,
       Fellowship we reap.

6   Fellowship is deepened
       Thru the cross of death;
    Fellowship is lifted
       By the Spirit's breath.

7   Fellowship will free us
       From our sinful self;
    Fellowship will bring us
       Into God Himself.

Composition for prophecy with main point and sub-points:

9/23/07 — Brother Benjamin

Matt: 7:1-12, 5:48; Luke 11:13
Rom: 8:4.

Christ as the life giving Spirit is living in us. We have received the divine life of Christ → we are the children of God. We are in the new testament - The Age of Grace. Christ is the real Sabbath. Peace and rest comes only through Christ. The old testament sabbath was fulfilled in Christ. 5:48 - be perfect as our heavenly father is perfect. Our Father (God) divine life is in us. We can only be perfect when we believe and receive Christ as our life. We can only fulfill the perfect life through the divine life of Christ living in us. - To express and fulfill God's purpose on earth.

In the divine life, there is no anxiety - If we live by our divine life ⟹ Transformation change in our nature and divine life → Renewal of our life.

The prayers → knock = Be specific to knock on the door! Be specific to God and expect an answer from the Lord that is specific.

If our eyes are single (looking to the Lord only) we can see purely focused on the Lord first with our heart turned and focused solely on the Lord.

Matth 7:11 The good things that God wants to give us is His Spirit (holy) - Himself to us as the life giving spirit ⟹ ALL SPIRITUAL BLESSINGS IN THE HEAVENLIES. God wants to possess and occupy our innermost being. to express Him as our life and living, to express and give His life to others.

Knowing the Triune God
by Experiencing and Enjoying Him

Scripture Reading: 1 John 1:1-3; 2:1, 27; 3:24; 4:9-10, 13-15; 2 John 8; 3 John 11

Day 1

I. **We come to know the Triune God by experiencing and enjoying Him (1 John 1:5; 2:27; 4:16; 5:11-12):**

  A. The concern of the apostle John in writing his Epistles was the experience and enjoyment of the Triune God (2 John 8).

  B. The Triune God is not merely the object of our faith; He is dwelling in us as our life and life supply for our experience and enjoyment (1 John 4:13-15).

  C. We need to know the Triune God experientially through the inner enjoyment of the subjective God (2:27; 4:4).

  D. If we would know the Triune God, we must be in the line of life and in the process of the growth in life; the more we grow in life, the more we will be concerned with the Divine Trinity (2:13-18).

II. **The Trinity of the Godhead is revealed more fully in the Gospel of John than any other place in the Bible; concerning this, 1 John is both a continuation and a development of the Gospel of John (John 14:6-24, 26; 15:26; 16:13-15; 1 John 3:24; 4:13-14; 5:11-12).**

Day 2

III. **The Epistles of John reveal the Triune God— the Father, the Son, and the Spirit (1 John 1:1-2; 2:23-24; 3:24; 4:2, 6, 13-14; 5:6, 11-12; 2 John 9):**

  A. To know God as the Father is to know Him as the source, the unique Initiator, the One who plans, originates, and initiates; everything originates with Him, and everything proceeds from Him (1 John 1:2-3; 2:13, 15; 3:1; 4:14; Matt. 15:13; Rom. 11:36; 1 Cor. 8:6; Eph. 3:14-16):

1. The Father is the source of the eternal life; from Him and with Him the Son was manifested as the expression of the eternal life for the people of the Father's choice to partake of and enjoy (1 John 1:2-3; 5:11-12).
2. The title *Father* refers to the impartation of life; through Christ's resurrection the Father imparts His life to His children (3:1; 1 Pet. 1:3).

B. In 1 John 1:1-2 both *the Word of life* and *life* denote the divine person of Christ the Son, who was with the Father in eternity and was manifested in time through incarnation (John 1:1, 14):

1. Christ the Son is the eternal, preexisting One who is from the beginning (1 John 2:13a, 14a).
2. The Son of God was manifested, that He might undo and destroy the works, the sinful deeds, of the devil (3:8b).
3. God sent His Son as a propitiation for our sins (4:10):
   a. Christ is the sacrifice for our propitiation before God (2:2).
   b. The Lord Jesus Christ offered Himself to God as a sacrifice for our sins (Heb. 9:28), not only for our redemption but also for the satisfying of God's demand, thus appeasing the relationship between us and God.

Day 3

4. God sent His only begotten Son into the world that we might have life and live through Him (1 John 4:9):
   a. The Son of God saves us not only from our sins by His blood but also from our death by His life (Eph. 1:7; 1 John 3:14-15; John 5:24).
   b. Christ is not only the Lamb of God who takes away our sin but also the Son of

God who gives us eternal life (1:29; 3:36;
10:10b).

5. The Son of God is the means through which
God gives us eternal life (1 John 5:11-12):
   a. Because the life is in the Son and the Son
   is the life, the Son and the life are one,
   inseparable (John 11:25; 14:6; Col. 3:4).
   b. He who has the Son has the life, and he
   who does not have the Son of God does
   not have the life (1 John 5:12).

6. Our Advocate with the Father is Jesus
Christ the Righteous; when we sin, the
Lord Jesus, based on the propitiation that
He accomplished, takes care of our case by
interceding and pleading for us (2:1; Rom.
8:34).

Day 4   C. The Spirit of truth in 1 John 4:6 is the Holy
Spirit, the Spirit of reality (John 14:17; 15:26;
16:13):

1. The Spirit is the reality; this means that
the Spirit is the reality of all that Christ as
the Son of God is (1 John 5:6).

2. By the Spirit whom God gave to us, we
know that the Triune God abides in us
(3:24).

D. First John 4:13-14 reveals that we are abiding
in God the Father and He in us, that God the
Father has given to us of His Spirit, and that
the Father has sent the Son as the Savior of the
world:

1. *Out of His Spirit* (lit.) in verse 13 implies
that the Spirit of God, whom God has given
to us, is bountiful and without measure; by
such a bountiful, immeasurable Spirit we
know with full assurance that we and God
are one and that we abide in each other
(Phil. 1:19; John 3:34).

2. Our God, the Father, has given us the
all-inclusive, life-giving Spirit, who is

the bountiful supply of Jesus Christ, the
Son (1 Cor. 15:45b; 2 Cor. 3:17).

IV. **The experience and enjoyment of the Triune
God has a focal point: God becoming man,
the God-man, and this God-man accomplishing redemption and in resurrection becoming the life-giving Spirit (1 John 4:9-10,
13-14; 1 Cor. 15:45b).**

V. **The Father, the Son, and the Spirit are one
yet are distinct in the Godhead but without
separation, for the Father, the Son, and the
Spirit coexist in the way of coinherence
(John 10:38; 14:10-11, 20; 17:21).**

Day 5 VI. **The Father, the Son, and the Spirit are all in
us, but from experience we know that we
have only One in us; this One who dwells in
us is the Triune God (Eph. 4:6; Col. 1:27; John
14:17; 1 John 4:13, 15).**

VII. **The anointing is the moving of the Triune
God experienced and enjoyed by us; the
teaching of the anointing is actually the
Triune God teaching us concerning Himself
(2:20, 27).**

VIII. **Eternal life is the Triune God whom we
experience in the fellowship of the divine
life, according to the divine anointing, and
by the virtues of the divine birth with the
divine seed (1:3, 7; 2:20, 27, 29; 3:9; 4:16).**

Day 6 IX. **To see God means to enjoy God and experience Him (3 John 11):**

A. We cannot see God without enjoying Him, and
we cannot know God without experiencing Him
(Job 42:5, footnote 1).

B. Knowing God and seeing God are a matter of
experiencing and enjoying Him; our experience
of God is our knowing of Him, and our enjoyment of God is our seeing of Him.

X. **When the Triune God becomes our experience and enjoyment, He is not only the One**

on the throne who is universally vast, but He
is also the One in our heart (Rev. 4:2-3; 5:6;
1 John 3:19-21):

A. We know the Triune God not in the vastness of
the universe but in the personal realm of our
heart (Heb. 8:10-11).

B. The concern of the New Testament is that we
know the Triune God who has come to dwell in
our being—the One who dwells in our spirit and
desires to spread into all the inward parts of our
heart (Eph. 3:14-17a; 1 John 3:19-21).

C. The New Testament way for us to know the
Triune God is personal, detailed, and experiential (2:20, 27; Heb. 10:16).

D. How precious is this experiential way of knowing the Triune God!

Morning Nourishment

1 John **And these things we write that our joy may be made**
1:4 **full.**
3:24 **And he who keeps His commandments abides in**
Him, and He in him. And in this we know that He
abides in us, by the Spirit whom He gave to us.
2 Cor. **The grace of the Lord Jesus Christ and the love of God**
13:14 **and the fellowship of the Holy Spirit be with you all.**

The first Epistle of John is both a continuation and a development of the Gospel of John. In the Gospel of John we see how to receive the divine life by believing in the Lord Jesus. However, in John's Gospel we cannot see much concerning how to enjoy what we have received of the divine life. Therefore, in 1 John, the apostle John gives us a continuation and development of his Gospel, showing us that after receiving the divine life we may enjoy the riches of the divine life. (*Life-study of 1 John,* pp. 30-31)

Today's Reading

[A subtlety of the enemy] is to deny that the Triune God is subjective to us for experience and enjoyment and to present the Divine Trinity merely as an objective doctrine for religion. The religion of many Christians is based on the creeds. In certain denominations the Apostles' Creed is recited in their services every week. Many of those who recite the creed have no experience of the Triune God. To them, the Divine Trinity is merely a belief in doctrine. But the Bible reveals that the Triune God is not merely the object of our faith; He is subjective to us, dwelling in us to be our life and life supply. Daily, even hourly, we need to experience Him and enjoy Him in this way. This is confirmed by the word concerning the enjoyment of the Triune God in 2 Corinthians 13:14.

The Bible reveals clearly that the Triune God, after passing through the process of incarnation, human living, crucifixion, resurrection, and ascension, has consummated in the all-inclusive Spirit, who has come to dwell in our spirit. Hallelujah for the wonderful all-inclusive Spirit dwelling in our human spirit! Our spirit may be a small organ, but this Spirit nonetheless dwells in it.

A human being can be compared to a transistor radio. Such a radio has a receiving apparatus that enables it to receive radio waves. When the radio is tuned properly, it will play music. We may say that we human beings are like transistor radios and that the receiving apparatus is our human spirit. When our receiver is properly tuned, we enjoy heavenly music. This is an illustration of the enjoyment of the Triune God, who is now the life-giving Spirit dwelling in our regenerated human spirit. This is the reason we stress the importance of the human spirit. It is by our spirit that we touch, enjoy, and experience the all-inclusive Spirit.

The fact that John's writing is based on the believers' growth in life should cause us to realize that if we would understand the Trinity, especially as the Divine Trinity is covered in this portion, we must be in the process of the growth in life,...in the line of life. If we are not in the line of life pursuing the growth in life, we shall not be able to understand anything concerning the Divine Trinity.

When the Triune God as revealed in this portion is ministered to believers who are not growing in life, they do not have any understanding or appreciation of what they hear. But when this is ministered to the seeking ones who are growing in life, they can understand what is ministered and are helped by it. They appreciate the "music" that is "played" concerning the Triune God. They are very responsive when we speak concerning the all-inclusive, compound, life-giving Spirit, who is the processed Triune God. However, those Christians who are not in the line of life and who are not growing in life may wonder what we mean by such terms as all-inclusive, compound, life-giving, and processed. Praise the Lord that we have the all-inclusive, compound, life-giving Spirit, who is the processed Triune God, living, moving, and working within us! When we hear the heavenly melody regarding this wonderful Triune God, we rejoice, and we are very happy in the Lord. (*Life-study of 1 John,* pp. 286-287, 167-168)

Further Reading: The Economy of God and the Mystery of the Transmission of the Divine Trinity, chs. 4-5

Enlightenment and inspiration: _____

_____

_____

_____

Morning Nourishment

1 John (And the life was manifested, and we have seen and
1:2-3   testify and report to you the eternal life, which was with
        the Father and was manifested to us); that which we
        have seen and heard we report also to you that you also
        may have fellowship with us, and indeed our fellow-
        ship is with the Father and with His Son Jesus Christ.
4:10   Herein is love, not that we have loved God but that He
        loved us and sent His Son as a propitiation for our sins.

First John 1:2 says that eternal life was with the Father....The
eternal life which is the Son was not only with the Father, but was
living and acting in union and communion with the Father in
eternity. This word corresponds to John 1:1-2....The Father is the
source of the eternal life, from whom and with whom the Son was
manifested as the expression of the eternal life for those the
Father has chosen to partake of and enjoy this life....John says
that the life which was with the Father was manifested to the
apostles. The manifestation of eternal life includes revelation and
impartation of life to men, with a view to bringing man into the
eternal life, into its union and communion with the Father.

[The Father] is the source of the divine life, the One of whom
we have been born with this life. The love of God is manifested by
sending His Son to die for us so that we may have His life and thus
become His children (4:9; John 3:16; 1:12-13). The sending of His
Son is for begetting us. Hence, the love of God is a begetting love,
particularly in the Father. (*Life-study of 1 John,* pp. 35-36, 224)

Today's Reading

In his first Epistle John says that God sent His Son as a propitiation for our sins (4:10). John also says that God sent His Son,
the only begotten, into the world that we may live through Him
and also that the Son may be the Savior of the world (4:9, 14).
In 3:8 John says that "the Son of God was manifested, that He
might destroy the works of the devil."

God sent His Son through incarnation....Incarnation is the
Son coming with the Father and by the Spirit to become a man.

According to the New Testament, the Lord Jesus was conceived of the Spirit and came with the Father. By this we see that the Trinity is involved with the incarnation. The issue of the incarnation ...was a wonderful man by the name of Jesus. Therefore, the incarnation was not an act merely of the Son, not an act that had nothing to do with the Father or the Spirit. Rather, when the Son was incarnated, He came with the Father and by the Spirit. Hence, the three of the Trinity—the Father, the Son, and the Spirit—all participated in the incarnation.

As God incarnate, the Lord Jesus lived on earth for thirty-three and a half years. Then He went to the cross and died for our redemption. In resurrection He became the life-giving Spirit.

In the Epistles of John the truth includes all these crucial matters concerning Christ's incarnation, human living, crucifixion, and resurrection,...[implying the elements of] divinity, humanity, incarnation, crucifixion, redemption, and resurrection. This truth implies all that the Triune God is, all that He has done, and all that He has obtained and attained. This all-inclusive reality is the truth that is the basic structure of John's Epistles.

The enemy brought in different heresies concerning the Person of Christ, [with] the intention...to distract people from the truth or confuse them with respect to the truth, with the result that the saints' enjoyment of the Triune God would be destroyed. ...John wrote his three Epistles to combat the work of the enemy.

We all must see the picture of the divine reality presented by John in his Epistles. This is a picture of the Triune God becoming our enjoyment through incarnation, human living, crucifixion, resurrection, and ascension. Whoever is against this enjoyment is a false prophet, a deceiver, an antichrist. But whoever is for the enjoyment of the Triune God is an honest and faithful worker for the truth, and we should be joined to that one and participate in his work. (*Life-study of 3 John*, pp. 16-17)

Further Reading: Life-study of 1 John, msgs. 2, 4; The Economy of God and the Mystery of the Transmission of the Divine Trinity, ch. 6

Enlightenment and inspiration: _____

_____

_____

_____

Morning Nourishment

1 John   And this is the testimony, that God gave to us eternal
5:11-12   life and this life is in His Son. He who has the Son has
          the life; he who does not have the Son of God does not
          have the life.

   3:14   We know that we have passed out of death into life
          because we love the brothers. He who does not love
          abides in death.

   2:1-2 My little children, these things I write to you that you
          may not sin. And if anyone sins, we have an Advocate
          with the Father, Jesus Christ the Righteous; and He
          Himself is the propitiation for our sins...

[In 1 John 5:11 and 12], the testimony of God is not only that
Jesus is His Son, but also that He gives to us eternal life, which is
in His Son. His Son is the means to give us His eternal life, which
is His goal with us. Because the life is in the Son (John 1:4) and
the Son is the life (John 11:25; 14:6; Col. 3:4), the Son and the life
are one, inseparable. (*Life-study of 1 John,* p. 324)

Today's Reading

Death [in 1 John 3:14] is of the devil, God's enemy Satan, signified by the tree of knowledge of good and evil, which brings death.
Life is of God, the source of life, signified by the tree of life, which
issues in life (Gen. 2:9, 16-17). Death and life are not only of these
two sources, Satan and God; they are also two essences, two elements, and two spheres. To pass out of death is to pass out of
the source, the essence, the element, and the sphere of death into the
source, the essence, the element, and the sphere of life. This took
place in us at our regeneration.

In 1 John 2:1 we have two important titles—Advocate and
Father. The title Father indicates that we are in the divine family
enjoying the Father's love. The title Advocate indicates that we
may be wrong in certain matters and need someone to take our
case. Hence, in family life we need our elder Brother to be our
Advocate who takes our case.

The truth in the Bible is always presented in a balanced way.

The truth in this verse is also balanced. On the one hand, the title Father is a sign of love; on the other hand, the title Advocate is a sign of righteousness. For example, a father loves his child. But if the child misbehaves, the father will have a case against him, a case based on righteousness. Although the child is still loved by his father and will continue to be taken care of by him, the father has a case against the child and may need to discipline him. In a similar way, whenever we sin, the Father has a case against us. Therefore, we need a heavenly attorney. We need Jesus Christ, our elder Brother, to be our Advocate.

According to John's word in 2:1 our Advocate with the Father is Jesus Christ the Righteous. Our Lord Jesus is the only righteous man among all men. His righteous act (Rom. 5:18) on the cross fulfilled the righteous requirement of the righteous God for us and all sinners. Only He is qualified to be our Advocate to care for us in our sinning condition and restore us to a righteous condition so that our Father, who is righteous, may be appeased.

Instead of saying "Jesus Christ the Righteous," we may say "Jesus Christ, the right One." Jesus Christ certainly is the One who is right, the right One, and only this right One can be our Advocate with the Father. The reason we have a problem and the Father has a case against us is that we are the wrong ones. Because we are the ones who are wrong, we need the righteous One to take care of our case.

In 1:7 we have the blood of Jesus; in 2:1 the Person of Christ as our Advocate; and…in 2:2 we have Christ as a propitiation concerning our sins. Our Advocate, who shed His blood for the cleansing of our sins, is our propitiation. This word "propitiation" indicates appeasing or peacemaking. When a child is wrong and his father has a case against him, there is no peace between them. In such a situation, there is the need of peacemaking and of appeasing the father. This peacemaking, this appeasing, is propitiation. (*Life-study of 1 John,* pp. 236, 115-116)

Further Reading: Life-study of 1 John, msgs. 13-14

Enlightenment and inspiration: _____

_____

_____

_____

Morning Nourishment

1 John **And as for you, the anointing which you have**
2:27 **received from Him abides in you, and you have no**
need that anyone teach you; but as His anointing
teaches you concerning all things and is true and is
not a lie, and even as it has taught you, abide in Him.

4:13-14 **In this we know that we abide in Him and He in us,**
that He has given to us of His Spirit. And we have
beheld and testify that the Father has sent the Son as
the Savior of the world.

John **But this He said concerning the Spirit, whom those**
7:39 **who believed into Him were about to receive; for** *the*
Spirit was not yet, because Jesus had not yet been
glorified.

In 1 John 2:27...I would call your attention to the pronouns "Him" (used twice) and "His." As [also is] the case in verse 25, these pronouns refer to both the Son and the Father,...[proving] that the Son and the Father are one.

It is significant that in these verses the pronoun "they" is not used with respect to the Father and the Son. Rather, John uses singular pronouns to refer to both the Son and the Father. Nevertheless, the expression "in the Son and in the Father" (v. 24) points to a distinction between the Son and the Father....Although there is a distinction between the Son and the Father, there is no separation, because the Father and the Son are one. Therefore the Father and the Son are distinct but inseparable. (*Life-study of 1 John,* p. 200)

Today's Reading

In the Epistles of John there is an underlying thought...related to the fact that at the time these Epistles were written certain heresies concerning the person of Christ had crept in. The effect of these heretical teachings was to annul the saints' enjoyment of the Triune God. This enjoyment has a focal point: God becoming man, and this God-man accomplishing redemption and in resurrection becoming the life-giving Spirit. (*Life-study of 3 John,* p. 15)

In 1 John 4:13 John...says that God "has given to us of His Spirit."

In Greek *of* literally means "out of." God has given us out of His Spirit. This closely resembles...the word in 3:24, which proves that this does not mean that God has given us something, such as the various gifts in 1 Corinthians 12:4, of His Spirit, but that His Spirit Himself is the all-inclusive gift (Acts 2:38). "Out of His Spirit" is an expression which implies that the Spirit of God, whom He has given to us, is bountiful and without measure (Phil. 1:19; John 3:34). By such a bountiful immeasurable Spirit we know with full assurance that we are one with God and that we abide in Him and He in us. (*Life-study of 1 John,* p. 305)

First John 4:13 and 14 show that we are abiding in God [the Father] and He in us, that God the Father has given us of His Spirit, and that the Father has sent the Son as the Savior of the world. Verse 13 says that God the Father has given us "of" His Spirit....What God has given us is the complete, consummated, all-inclusive, compound, life-giving, indwelling, processed Spirit. Our God, the Father, has given us of this all-inclusive Spirit, who is the bountiful supply of Jesus Christ, the Son. (*Living in and with the Divine Trinity,* p. 54)

After the Son died on the cross and was buried, in resurrection He became the life-giving Spirit. This means that the Father is in the Son and that the Son became the life-giving Spirit. This is the Spirit spoken of in John 7:39....Now when we preach the gospel concerning Christ the Son and people believe in Him and call on His name, they receive not only the Son, but also the Father and the Spirit, for all three are one. The Son came with the Father, and the Spirit comes not only with the Son but as the reality of the Son with the Father. We need to be clear that the Son came with the Father and the Spirit came not only with the Son but as the reality of the Son. Furthermore, all three—the Father, the Son, and the Spirit—coinhere. This is the Triune God—the Father, the Son, and the Spirit as the one God—as revealed in the Bible....When the Triune God reaches us today, He comes as the Spirit. (*Life-study of 1 John,* pp. 282-283)

Further Reading: Life-study of 3 John, msg. 2; *Life-study of 1 John,* msg. 32

Enlightenment and inspiration: _____

_____

_____

_____

Morning Nourishment

1 John And as for you, the anointing which you have
2:27 received from Him abides in you, and you have no
need that anyone teach you; but as His anointing
teaches you concerning all things and is true and is
not a lie, and even as it has taught you, abide in Him.
4:15-16 Whoever confesses that Jesus is the Son of God, God
abides in him and he in God. And we know and have
believed the love which God has in us. God is love,
and he who abides in love abides in God and God
abides in him.

The Triune God, who is now organically one with us, is teaching us concerning Himself [1 John 2:27]. This teaching is subjective and experiential. Day by day, as we are in the organic union with the Triune God, we enjoy Him, we experience Him, and we live in Him, with Him, and by Him. This living is a constant teaching of the things concerning the Triune God. We can testify that we certainly enjoy the Triune God in our daily life. (*Life-study of 1 John*, p. 181)

Today's Reading

We may use eating food as an illustration of learning the things of the Triune God in the way of enjoying and experiencing Him. The best way to know a certain kind of food is to eat that food. If you eat the food, you will be taught concerning the food by the very food you eat. This is not merely an objective lesson concerning food; it is a subjective knowing of the food through experience. The more you eat a particular food, the more you will come to know it. This knowledge is not doctrinal; it is experiential. In a similar way, we come to know the Triune God by enjoying and experiencing Him. It is impossible for us to know the Triune God merely by doctrine. But we can know Him by enjoying and experiencing Him.

When the Triune God becomes our enjoyment and experience, His moving is the anointing within us. This understanding enables us to give a proper definition of the anointing: the anointing is the moving of the Triune God becoming our inward enjoyment and experience.

We need to be impressed with the fact that the anointing is the moving of the Triune God enjoyed and experienced by us.... The anointing here in chapter two of 1 John refers to our experience of the Triune God. It is this experience that teaches us the things concerning the Trinity.

John's word concerning the anointing here was written to the young children, to those who are the youngest in the divine life. Even the youngest believers have experienced the Lord within them. They can testify from their experience that the One who lives in them is the Father, the Son, and the Spirit.

In chapter two of 1 John we certainly have the compound ointment, the all-inclusive Spirit. However, here we do not have the ointment merely in an objective way; instead, we have the subjective anointing, that is, the subjective moving and working of the ointment. This subjective anointing is the processed Triune God experienced by us. Furthermore, this anointing teaches us concerning the processed Triune God. For example, if someone should say that Christ is not in us, we should reply, "From my experience of the anointing I know that Jesus Christ is in me." Moreover, if someone should try to teach you that the Father, the Son, and the Spirit are three separate persons, you may say, "I don't have three separate persons within me. From my experience of the anointing I know that I have only One in me, and this One is the Father, the Son, and the Spirit."

The anointing is the moving of the Triune God within us. This means that our God has become subjective to us. The Triune God—the Father, the Son, and the Spirit—is within our spirit. Day by day this processed Triune God as the anointing leads us into the virtues of the divine life, the virtues we have received through the divine birth. These virtues include living a righteous life, loving the brothers, and overcoming all negative things. (*Life-study of 1 John,* pp. 181-182, 192-193, 232)

Further Reading: Life-study of 1 John, msgs. 21-22

Enlightenment and inspiration: _____

_____

_____

_____

Morning Nourishment

Job   I had heard of You by the hearing of the ear, / But
42:5   now my eye has seen You.
3 John   ...He who does good is of God; he who does evil has
11   not seen God.
1 John   Because if our heart blames *us, it is* because God is
3:20-21   greater than our heart and knows all things.
Beloved, if our heart does not blame *us,* we have
boldness toward God.

In the New Testament sense, seeing God equals gaining God. To gain God is to receive God in His element, in His life, and in His nature that we may be constituted with God. All God's redeemed, regenerated, sanctified, transformed, conformed, and glorified people will see God's face (Rev. 22:4). Seeing God transforms us (2 Cor. 3:18; cf. 1 John 3:2), because in seeing God we receive His element into us and our old element is discharged. This metabolic process is transformation (Rom. 12:2). To see God is to be transformed into the glorious image of Christ, the God-man, that we may express God in His life and represent Him in His authority. (Job 42:5, footnote)

Today's Reading

In 3 John 11, to see God actually means to enjoy God and experience Him. We cannot see God without enjoying Him, and we cannot know God without experiencing Him. Seeing and knowing God are a matter of enjoying and experiencing Him.

Recently I have been encouraged by many of the testimonies given by young saints in the meetings. These testimonies indicate that these young saints are enjoying God and experiencing Him. This also indicates that they have seen God and have known Him....Our testimonies indicate whether or not we are enjoying and experiencing God. As we have pointed out, our enjoyment of God is our seeing of Him, and our experience of God is our knowing of Him. (*Life-study of 3 John,* p. 14)

Christians often talk about knowing God. However, their concept is that of objective knowledge of a God who is great and almighty. But [in 1 John 3:21] the apostle John does not teach us to know God in that kind of objective way. On the contrary, John's word here is about knowing God in a very subjective way. Some may speak about the almighty God who rules the universe, but here John speaks concerning the God who is in our heart. He does not talk about the mighty God, about the great God; instead he speaks concerning the practical God. Not only is God infinite, unlimited, and beyond our ability to comprehend; He is also small enough to be in our heart. When God becomes our experience, He is not only the One on the throne who is universally vast, but He is the One in our heart.

Some have said, "How is it possible for Christ to be in you? Christ is great, and you are small. How could you contain such a great Christ?" This kind of talk comes from the fallen human mentality. According to the teaching of the New Testament, we need to know God in the personal realm of our heart. God is known by us not in the vastness of the universe, but in the smallness of our heart.

The concern of the New Testament is that we know the God who has come into our being, the One who dwells in our spirit and desires to spread into all the inward parts of our heart. Therefore, we need to know God in our heart.

In 3:20 John does not say that God is greater than the universe. Here John says that God is greater than our heart. This way of writing indicates that our knowledge of God must be experiential. Knowing God is a matter not of the universe but of our heart. Is your heart at peace? Is your heart tranquil? This is related to your knowing God. Some may say that they know God. But they may know Him in a religious way, in an objective way. We need to know God in our heart, in our conscience.

The New Testament way for us to know God is personal, detailed, and experiential. The New Testament way is to know God as the One who is in our heart. How precious is this experiential way of knowing God! (*Life-study of 1 John,* pp. 255-256, 258)

Further Reading: Life-study of 1 John, msgs. 28-29

Enlightenment and inspiration: _____

_____

_____

_____

Hymns, #1193

1   Life is God the Father in Christ Jesus
    As the Spirit flowing into us.
    How enjoyable, this Person wonderful!
    He's our life so rich and bountiful.

2   We experienced regeneration
    When we opened to this living One.
    We were born again; another life came in.
    Now it floods us till we're full of Him.

3   He within us is the living Spirit
    In our spirit, flowing out of it
    Into all our heart, transforming every part
    By the life which He Himself imparts.

4   Now He must have our cooperation.
    We must set our mind upon the Son.
    We must turn away from all that leads astray,
    Till our mind is set on Him each day.

5   Lord, our human spirit now contains You.
    Still Your purpose in us You would do;
    If our wandering mind would leave old
            thoughts behind,
    Then Your life and peace in it we'll find.

6   Lord, we would our every thought be captured
    By the rich enjoyment in Your Word.
    In it we're supplied, our mind there will abide,
    Till our thoughts are wholly sanctified.

7   Let's keep practicing the application
    Of this life by minding just the Son.
    Praise Him for the way to live by Him today!
    Lord, on You our minds will ever stay.

Composition for prophecy with main point and sub-points: _____

_____
_____
_____
_____
_____
_____
_____
_____
_____
_____
_____
_____
_____
_____
_____
_____
_____
_____
_____
_____
_____
_____
_____
_____
_____
_____
_____
_____
_____
_____
_____
_____
_____
_____
_____
_____

The Divine Revelation
of the Eternal Life for Our Enjoyment

Scripture Reading: 1 John 1:1-3; 2:25; 3:15; 5:11-13, 20

Day 1 I. **The Lord's recovery today is in the time of the mending ministry of John, mending the rents in the church by the ministry of life for God's building in life; the focus of John's writings is the mysteries of the divine life (Matt. 4:21; John 1:4; 10:10b; 14:6a; 1 John 1:1-3; 2:25; 3:15; 5:11-13, 20):**

A. John's Gospel, as the consummation of the Gospels, unveils the mysteries of the person and work of the Lord Jesus as the manifestation of the divine life.

B. John's Epistles (especially the first), as the consummation of the Epistles, unfold the mystery of the fellowship of the manifested divine life.

C. John's Revelation, as the consummation of the entire Bible, reveals the mystery of Christ as the life supply to God's children for His expression and as the center of the universal administration of the Triune God.

D. The way of the Lord's recovery is the way of life; we need to know the intrinsic essence of life in the Lord's recovery (John 1:4; 10:10b; 14:6a; 1 Cor. 15:45b; 1 John 1:1-3; 5:11-13; Rom. 8:2, 10, 6, 11).

Day 2 II. **The eternal life is the life "which is really life" (1 Tim. 6:19b):**

A. Life is not devotion:
  1. Devotion is our exercise of piety.
  2. Life is Christ living in us (Gal. 2:20a).

B. Life is not good behavior:
  1. Good behavior is our doing.
  2. Life is Christ lived out from us (Phil. 1:21a).

C. Life is not power:
  1. Power is for work (Acts 1:8).
  2. Life is for living (John 6:57b).

　　　D. Life is not gift:
　　　　1. Gift is the ability for function (Rom. 12:6).
　　　　2. Life is the Divine Being in our being (John
　　　　　 1:13b).

Day 3　　E. Life is not the growth in knowledge:
　　　　1. The growth in knowledge is the increase in
　　　　　 knowledge.
　　　　2. Life is the increase of God (Col. 2:19b).
　　　F. Life is not our human life:
　　　　1. Our human life (*bios* and *psuche*) is mortal
　　　　　 (Luke 8:43b; 21:4b; Matt. 16:25-26).
　　　　2. Life (*zoe*) is eternal (1 John 1:2; Psa. 90:2b).
　　　G. Life is God's content and God's flowing out:
　　　　1. God's content is God's being (Eph. 4:18a).
　　　　2. God's flowing out is the impartation of life
　　　　　 to us (Rev. 22:1).
　　　H. Life is Christ (John 14:6a; Col. 3:4a; 1 John 5:12a):
　　　　1. Christ is the embodiment of God, who is life
　　　　　 (Col. 2:9).
　　　　2. Christ is the expression of God (John 1:18;
　　　　　 Heb. 1:3a).
　　　I. Life is the Holy Spirit:
　　　　1. The Holy Spirit is the reality of Christ
　　　　　 (John 14:16-18; 1 Cor. 15:45b).
　　　　2. The Holy Spirit is the Spirit of life giving
　　　　　 life to us (Rom. 8:2a; 2 Cor. 3:6b).
　　　J. Life is the Triune God dispensed into us and
　　　　living in us:
　　　　1. God the Father is the source of life (John
　　　　　 5:26), God the Son is the embodiment of
　　　　　 life (1:4), and God the Spirit is the flow
　　　　　 of life (4:14b).
　　　　2. God the Father is the light of life (Rev. 21:23;
　　　　　 22:5), God the Son is the tree of life (v. 2),
　　　　　 and God the Spirit is the river of life (v. 1).

Day 4
&
Day 5　III. **Christ as the Word of life, the eternal life,**
　　　was manifested through incarnation as
　　　the embodiment of the Triune God to make
　　　God contactable, touchable, receivable,

experienceable, enterable, and enjoyable
(1 John 1:1-2; John 1:14):

A. The eternal life, which is the Son, not only was
   with the Father but also was living and acting in
   communion with the Father in eternity (1 John
   1:1-2; John 1:1-2).

B. The eternal life was manifested to the apostles, who saw, testified, and reported this life to
   people; the manifestation of the eternal life
   includes the revelation and impartation of
   life to men, with a view to bringing man into
   the eternal life, into its union and communion
   with the Father (1 John 1:1-3).

C. The eternal life was promised by God, released
   through Christ's death, and imparted to the believers through Christ's resurrection (2:25; John
   3:14-15; 12:24; cf. Luke 12:49-50; 1 Pet. 1:3).

D. The eternal life was received by the believers
   through believing in the Son; after the believers receive eternal life, this life becomes their
   life (John 3:15-16, 36; Col. 3:4a; John 1:12-13).

E. The believers are being saved in the eternal life
   to reign in this life (Rom. 5:10, 17).

F. The believers need to lay hold on the eternal
   life in this age so that they may inherit eternal life in the manifestation of the kingdom (1 Tim.
   6:12, 19; Matt. 19:17; Luke 18:29-30; Rev. 2:7).

G. The believers will fully enjoy eternal life in eternity (22:1-2, 14, 17, 19).

Day 6   **IV. When we are in the fellowship, the enjoy-
          ment, of God as the eternal life, we partake
          of God in His divine nature (2 Pet. 1:4) as
          Spirit, love, and light; Spirit is the nature of
          God's person (John 4:24), love is the nature
          of God's essence (1 John 4:8, 16), and light is
          the nature of God's expression (1:5):**

          A. If we spend an adequate amount of personal
             time with the Lord and remain in the fellowship
             with Him daily and hourly, we will enjoy the

Lord as the Spirit, and we will become persons who are full of the divine love (the inner substance of God) and the divine light (the expressed element of God) (v. 3; 2 Cor. 13:14):

1. The divine love is God Himself poured out in our hearts through the Holy Spirit to be the source for our enjoyment of the dispensing of the Triune God and the motivating power within us, that we may more than conquer over all our circumstantial situations (Rom. 5:5; 8:37, 39).

2. The divine light is the divine life in the Son operating in us; this light shines in the darkness within us, and the darkness cannot overcome it (John 1:4-5; 1 John 1:5).

B. When we enjoy God by touching God and being infused with God in the divine fellowship, we walk, live, move, and have our being in His Spirit as our person, in His love as our essence, and in His light as our expression for us to be His corporate testimony (Rom. 8:4; Eph. 5:2, 8; Matt. 5:14-16).

Morning Nourishment

1 John
1:1
That which was from the beginning, which we have heard, which we have seen with our eyes, which we beheld and our hands handled, concerning the Word of life.

John's ministry was not only to mend the broken ministry of Paul but also to consummate the entire divine revelation of both the Old Testament and the New Testament, of both the Gospels and the Epistles. In such a ministry, the focus is the mysteries of the divine life. John's Gospel, as the consummation of the Gospels, unveils the mysteries of the person and work of the Lord Jesus Christ. John's Epistles (especially the first), as the consummation of the Epistles, unfold the mystery of the fellowship of the divine life, which is the fellowship of God's children with God the Father and with one another. Then John's Revelation, as the consummation of the [entire Bible], reveals the mystery of Christ as the life supply to God's children for His expression and as the center of the universal administration of the Triune God. Here John used the expression *that which* to open his Epistle and unfold the mystery of the fellowship in the divine life. That he did not use personal pronouns in reference to the Lord implies that what he was about to unfold is mysterious. (1 John 1:1, footnote 1)

From the beginning...indicates that John's Epistle is a continuation of his Gospel [John 1:1], which concerns the believers' experience of the divine life. In his Gospel, John revealed the way for sinners to receive the eternal life—to believe in the Son of God. In his Epistle he pointed out the way for the believers, who have received the divine life, to enjoy that life in its fellowship—to abide in the Son of God. And in his Revelation he unveiled the consummation of the eternal life as the believers' full enjoyment in eternity. (1 John 1:1, footnote 2)

Today's Reading

The last hymn in our hymnal, #1348, is a wrong hymn based upon our present realization. This hymn is comprised of Revelation 21:3-4....[However, these verses] were spoken to the unbelievers who are the descendants of the sheep in Matthew 25:31-46. Revelation 21:5 through 7 refers to the sons of God, all the saints, the divinely saved ones through the generations....For God to wipe away tears with no sorrow or crying or pain are the blessings outside the city without eternal life [v. 4]. These are the blessings rendered to the unbelieving, God-created and restored people. These are the nations, not the sons of God. We are the sons of God....When we get into the New Jerusalem we will no longer be the old creation and there will be no tears. The restored nations, however, are still in the old creation. They still will have tears. The blessings to them will be that God will wipe away their tears. You may think this is an intimate blessing and that if God would wipe away your tears this would be marvelous. This indicates that you have never gotten into the blessing of the eternal life. The blessing of the eternal life is not to wipe away your tears but to fill you with another kind of water. If you are filled within with the living water, tears would never come out.

The fact that this hymn made it into our supplement shows that with just a little carelessness something is able to creep in.... We do need a controlling constitution that will rule out many things such as hymn #1348....Some teachings have gone out in the same principle. They were not in the intrinsic essence of the Lord's vision in His recovery....The principle of life has been changed and eventually "the mustard seed" will grow not into an herb but into a big tree. It will not be an herb for feeding people but a big tree for lodging evil things and evil persons.

We must be on the alert....We should not think that we are okay and that we are safeguarded. We all must take heed to our own preaching, our own teaching, our own so-called ministry. We must ask whether the principle of life has been changed or not. We must know the intrinsic essence of life in the Lord's recovery. (*Elders' Training, Book 2: The Vision of the Lord's Recovery,* pp. 72-74)

Further Reading: Life-study of 1 John, msg. 2; *Elders' Training, Book 2: The Vision of the Lord's Recovery,* ch. 6

Enlightenment and inspiration: _____

_____

_____

_____

Morning Nourishment

1 Tim. **Laying away for themselves a good foundation as**
6:19 **a treasure for the future, that they may lay hold on**
that which is really life.

The first point we need to see is that life is not devotion. Many Christians consider devotion to be the spiritual life, but devotion is our exercise of piety. It is an exercise on our side by our own effort. Paul said in Galatians 2:20a, "I am crucified with Christ; and it is no longer I who live, but it is Christ who lives in me." This shows that life is Christ living within us. We need to help the saints to realize that we should never consider devotion as life. One may be very devotional and yet not have much life. Some nuns and priests in the Catholic Church may be very devotional, but that is merely their kind of pious exercise. Life is not any kind of activity. Life is altogether Christ Himself. We must stress this to the uttermost, helping the saints to know that life is Christ Himself. Nothing can replace life. (*Basic Lessons on Life,* p. 55)

Today's Reading

Generally speaking, Christians consider that if a person's behavior is good, he has life. When I was in China, I observed that a number of the disciples of Confucius behaved better than the Christian missionaries. They were so gentle, patient, and humble. They were also very meek, having the virtue of giving in to others. But this is not life. This is merely good behavior....We need to stress that life is not good behavior....Life is Christ.

Man was created good, but man was corrupted and damaged by the fall. Still there is something good within man which was created by God. The teachings of Confucius are to help develop man's good nature, the natural, good virtues created by God within man. These virtues have been damaged but are still left in man's nature. The good behavior developed by man is according to his doing, but life is Christ lived out from us. Life is not our doing. Paul said in Philippians 1:21a, "For to me, to live is Christ." Thus, life is not good behavior; it is Christ lived out of us. First, Christ lives within us, and then Christ lives Himself out of us. This is life.

We have to train the saints to discern the difference between good behavior and life. We may admire a certain brother because he is gentle, meek, humble, and patient,...[thinking] that he is full of life, but...this brother whom we admire may be expressing his natural virtues in his good behavior. Life, however, is Christ expressed from within us and lived out from within us.

We also need to see that life is not power. The Spirit has two aspects: the aspect of life within us and the aspect of power upon us. When the New Testament talks about the Spirit's power, it uses the preposition *upon*. *Upon* means outside. When the New Testament speaks concerning the Spirit as life, it uses the preposition *in*. The Spirit is in us.

The New Testament says that the Spirit of reality will be with you and even in you, and the rivers of living water will flow out from within you. There is the aspect of drinking the Spirit and the aspect of being baptized in the Spirit. To baptize a person is to put him into the water, but to drink is to take in the water. First Corinthians 12:13 covers these two aspects. We all have been baptized in one Spirit into one Body. Then we all have been given to drink of one Spirit. These are the two aspects concerning the Spirit. But in today's Christianity the life side is nearly neglected, and the power side is overemphasized wrongly. Therefore, we have to point out that life is not power.

Acts 1:8 shows that the Spirit of power coming upon the disciples enabled them to carry out the work of spreading the gospel from Jerusalem to the uttermost part of the earth. This verse shows us that power is for work, and John 6:57b shows that life is for living. In this verse the Lord said, "He who eats Me, he also shall live because of Me."

Life is not gift. Gift is the ability for function (Rom. 12:6), but life is the Divine Being in our being. John 1:13b says that we believers are begotten of God....Life is God Himself, the Divine Being, in our being. (*Basic Lessons on Life*, pp. 55-57)

Further Reading: Basic Lessons on Life, lsn. 7

Enlightenment and inspiration: _____

_____

_____

_____

Morning Nourishment

Eph. **Being darkened in their understanding, alienated**
4:18 **from the life of God...**
Rev. **And he showed me a river of water of life, bright as**
22:1-2 **crystal, proceeding out of the throne of God and of the**
Lamb in the middle of its street. And on this side and
on that side of the river was the tree of life, producing
twelve fruits, yielding its fruit each month; and the
leaves of the tree are for the healing of the nations.

The growth in knowledge is not life. The growth in knowledge is the increase of knowledge. You may accumulate a lot of
biblical knowledge by reading books or by studying in a semi-
nary and yet not know life at all. Life is the increase of God
within us. Colossians 2:19b reveals that the church grows with
the growth of God, with the increase of God as life.

Our human life is not the life on which the Bible focuses. Our
human life (*bios* and *psuche*) is mortal (Luke 8:43b; 21:4b; Matt.
16:25-26). Our human life is not life because it dies and is destined
to die. The real life is immortal. Whatever is mortal is not life.
Both our physical life (*bios*) and our soulish life (*psuche*) are mortal,
so the human life is not life. In Luke 8:43b and 21:4b the Greek
word for "livelihood" and "living" is *bios*. *Bios* refers to the physical
life. In Matthew 16:25-26 the Greek word for "soul-life" is *psuche*.

Life (*zoe*) is eternal. Eternal means immortal. First John 1:2
says, "And the life was manifested, and we have seen and testify
and report to you the eternal life, which was with the Father and
was manifested to us." Then Psalm 90:2b says, "Indeed from
eternity to eternity, You are God." Strictly speaking, all lives that
are mortal are not life. The real life is immortal and eternal, and
this real life is God Himself because God is from eternity to eternity. God is eternal, so only God Himself is the real life. (*Basic
Lessons on Life*, pp. 57-58)

Today's Reading

The six foregoing points tell us what is not life. Now we need
to see what life is. Life is God's content and God's flowing out.

God's content is God's being, so life is God's inner being (Eph. 4:18a). God's flowing out is the impartation of Himself as life to us. In Revelation 22:1 we see the river of water of life flowing out from the throne of God. This is God's flowing out. Life is God's content, His inner being, and life is God flowing out into us and being imparted into our being.

We need to impress the saints that life is Christ (John 14:6a; Col. 3:4a; 1 John 5:12a). Christ is the embodiment of God, who is life. Colossians 2:9 says that all the fullness of the Godhead dwells in Christ bodily. God as life is embodied in Christ, and Christ is the expression of God. John 1:18 says that no one has ever seen God, but the only Begotten has declared Him. Then Hebrews 1:3 shows that Christ is the effulgence of God's glory. This means that Christ is the expression of God, who is life.

Finally, we need to point out that life is the Holy Spirit. The Holy Spirit is the reality of Christ (John 14:16-17; 1 Cor. 15:45b). The Son is the embodiment of the Father, and the Spirit is the reality of the Son. Romans 8:2a uses the term *the Spirit of life,* and 2 Corinthians 3:6b says that the Spirit gives life. Thus, the Holy Spirit today is the Spirit of life who gives life to us. We must stress that the Spirit in the New Testament has two aspects. On the one hand, He is the Spirit of power; on the other hand, He is the Spirit of life.

We need to pay attention to the focus of this message: life is the Triune God dispensed into us and living in us. The Father is the source, the Son is the course, and the Spirit is the flow. The Triune God is dispensed into us in His Divine Trinity and is now living within us.

Such a lesson on the definition of life is greatly needed among us. We may use the term *life,* and yet not know what life is. We have to enter into a full understanding of what life is. (*Basic Lessons on Life,* pp. 58-59)

Further Reading: Basic Lessons on Life, lsn. 7; *The Mending Ministry of John,* ch. 6

Enlightenment and inspiration: _____

_____

_____

_____

Morning Nourishment

1:1-3   t which was from the beginning, which we
        e heard, which we have seen with our eyes,
        which we beheld and our hands handled, concern-
        ing the Word of life (and the life was manifested,
        and we have seen and testify and report to you the
        eternal life, which was with the Father and was
        manifested to us); that which we have seen and
        heard we report also to you that you also may have
        fellowship with us, and indeed our fellowship is
        with the Father and with His Son Jesus Christ.
John   In the beginning was the Word, and the Word was
1:1-2   with God, and the Word was God. He was in the
        beginning with God.

The Father is the source of the eternal life, from whom and with whom the Son was manifested as the expression of the eternal life for those the Father has chosen to partake of and enjoy this life.

John says that the life which was with the Father was manifested to the apostles. The manifestation of eternal life includes revelation and impartation of life to men, with a view to bringing man into the eternal life, into its union and communion with the Father.

What was once hidden has been manifested to the apostles. John, one of the apostles, now opens to us the divine mysteries. If we eat the Word through pray-reading, we shall receive the benefit of the manifestation of eternal life. (*Life-study of 1 John*, pp. 35-36)

Today's Reading

The eternal life was promised by God. First John 2:25 says, "And this is the promise which He Himself promised us, the eternal life." In the Gospel of John eternal life is promised in such verses as 3:15; 4:14; and 10:10. In Titus 1:2 Paul speaks of "the hope of eternal life, which God, who cannot lie, promised before the times of the ages." This promise of eternal life must be the promise made by the Father to the Son in eternity. It must have been that in eternity past the Father promised the Son that He would give His eternal life to His believers.

Eternal life was not only promised and manifested; it was also released through Christ's death (John 3:14-15). The divine life was concealed, confined, in Christ. But through His death this divine life was released from within Him.

The eternal life that was released from within Christ through His death has been imparted into the believers through His resurrection. Concerning this, 1 Peter 1:3 says, "Blessed be the God and Father of our Lord Jesus Christ, who according to His great mercy has regenerated us unto a living hope through the resurrection of Jesus Christ from the dead."

The eternal life that has been released through Christ's death and imparted through His resurrection has been received by the believers through their believing in the Son. According to John 3:15-16 and 36, everyone who believes in the Son has eternal life.

After the believers receive eternal life, this life becomes their life (Col. 3:4). This is the purpose of God's salvation, that is, to make His life our life so that we may become His children, partaking of His divine nature to enjoy all that He is and to live a life that expresses Him.

In Romans 5:10 Paul says, "For if we, being enemies, were reconciled to God through the death of His Son, much more we will be saved in His life, having been reconciled." Reconciliation to God through Christ has been accomplished already, but being saved in His life from so many negative things is still a daily matter. Day by day we may be saved in the eternal life. (*Life-study of 1 John,* pp. 36-38)

Further Reading: Life-study of 1 John, msgs. 3-4; *Crystallization-study of the Epistle to the Romans,* msg. 6

Enlightenment and inspiration: _____

_____

_____

_____

Morning Nourishment

1 Tim. **Fight the good fight of the faith; lay hold on the eter-**
6:12 **nal life, to which you were called and have confessed**
      the good confession before many witnesses.
Matt. **And everyone who has left houses or brothers or sis-**
19:29 **ters or father or mother or children or fields for My**
      name's sake shall receive a hundred times as much
      and shall inherit eternal life.

[Romans 5:17 says], "…Those who receive the abundance of grace and of the gift of righteousness will reign in life through the One, Jesus Christ." Having the divine life within us, we may be saved by this life and also reign in it. We can be kings ruling in the divine life over all negative things. For example,…many of us would say, "Instead of ruling like a king over my temper, my temper has been ruling me." The reason many saints cannot rule their temper is that they do not enjoy eternal life. Do not make up your mind and strongly decide that from now on you will never lose your temper. That way does not work. Instead, forget about your temper and feast on this life. I would encourage you to mingle the calling on the name of the Lord with the pray-reading of the Word. If you do this, you will enjoy the Lord. As you enjoy Him, He will be the One reigning over all the negative things. Then as He reigns within you, you will reign in His reigning. This is the proper way to reign in life over your temper. (*Life-study of 1 John,* p. 38)

Today's Reading

You cannot reign over your temper simply by learning the doctrines and teachings of the Bible. When some hear this, they may say, "You ignore Bible doctrine and uplift calling on the Lord and eating the Word. According to you, we can be overcomers by this calling and eating." I would reply by asking these ones how much they have been helped by doctrines and teachings to overcome their temper. Many of those who know the doctrines of the Bible still lose their temper again and again.

As believers, we should lay hold on eternal life. In 1 Timothy 6:12 Paul charges us to "lay hold on the eternal life, to which you were called." In 1 Timothy 6:19 he urges us to "lay hold on that which is really life." This life is the eternal life. To lay hold on eternal life means that in everything—in our daily life, in our ministry, and in our jobs—we need to attach ourselves to the divine life and to apply the divine life to every situation, not trusting in our human life.

In Matthew 19:29 the Lord Jesus speaks of inheriting eternal life. To inherit eternal life is to be rewarded in the coming age with the enjoyment of the divine life in the manifestation of the kingdom of the heavens. Certain believers who have received eternal life enjoy it to some extent; however, they do not enjoy it to the proper extent. As a result, when the Lord Jesus comes back at the time of the manifestation of the kingdom, they will miss the enjoyment of the millennial kingdom;...[they will] miss the enjoyment of eternal life during that dispensation.

In eternity all believers will fully enjoy eternal life. According to Revelation 22:1 and 2, in the New Jerusalem all the believers will enjoy the divine life as the flowing river and as the growing tree. Both the river and the tree are for our eternal enjoyment. For eternity, we shall enjoy this divine life (Rev. 22:14, 17, 19).

Eternal life is related to the present age, to the coming age of the kingdom, and to the eternal age. In the present age we receive the divine life and live the divine life. If we live this life according to the Lord's desire, we shall also enjoy the divine life in the coming age of the kingdom. Eventually, all believers will enjoy eternal life to the uttermost in the eternal age. However, if those who receive eternal life in this age do not live it properly but instead neglect it, then in the coming age, the age of the kingdom, they will miss the enjoyment of the divine life. By missing the enjoyment of eternal life in the kingdom age, they will learn certain lessons and be trained. Eventually they will be restored to the enjoyment of the eternal life. Then ultimately, in the eternal age, all believers will have the full enjoyment of the divine life. (*Life-study of 1 John*, pp. 38-40)

Further Reading: A Brief Presentation of the Lord's Recovery, pp. 19-22;
Elders' Training, Book 2: The Vision of the Lord's Recovery, ch. 5

Enlightenment and inspiration: _____

_____

_____

_____

Morning Nourishment

John 4:24	**God is Spirit, and those who worship Him must worship in spirit and truthfulness.**
1 John 4:16	**...God is love, and he who abides in love abides in God and God abides in him.**
1:5	**And this is the message which we have heard from Him and announce to you, that God is light and in Him is no darkness at all.**

We believers have all been made partakers of this divine nature (2 Pet. 1:4). It is a very hard task to define the divine nature. Simply speaking, the divine nature is what God is, just as the nature of anything is what that thing is....The Bible tells us that God is Spirit (John 4:24), that God is love (1 John 4:8, 16), and that God is light (1 John 1:5). Then in a total way the Bible tells us that God is life (John 1:4; 5:26; 14:6). These four items of what God is are very basic. Spirit, love, and light are the very constituents of God's being and life is God Himself. God Himself, God's being, is our life, and He is constituted with Spirit, love, and light. Spirit is the nature of God's person, love is the nature of God's essence, and light is the nature of God's expression.

God is Spirit in person, God is love in essence, God is light in expression, and God is life in love as its essence and in light as its expression. When we touch God, we touch Him as Spirit in His person, as love in His essence, and as light in His expression. After touching God, we walk, we live, we have our being, in His Spirit as our person, in His love as our essence, and in His light as our expression. (*God's New Testament Economy*, p. 319)

Today's Reading

In 1 John we first see the eternal life...as the Word of life. Then John testified and reported to us the eternal life that we may have fellowship (1:1-3). John's first Epistle mainly is to keep us living in the divine fellowship of the divine life. As believers we have the divine life, and this life brings us into the divine fellowship. We all need to remain in the fellowship. If we remain in the fellowship, we touch God as light (1 John 1:5) and as love (1 John 4:8-16). This is our enjoyment of God as light and love in our fellowship with Him....To partake of the divine nature is to fellowship with God, to enjoy God as love and as light, because love and light are two constituents of God's nature.

If you spend ten or fifteen minutes to contact the Lord and stay with Him and pray honestly and sincerely, confessing your failures, mistakes, shortcomings, defects, wrongdoings, and sinfulness, you touch God as the Spirit in His person. Deep within your being you sense the Spirit. At this juncture everything in your home, in your yard, on the street, in the heavens, and on the earth is so pleasant and lovely. This is the issue of partaking of love as the nature of God's essence.

All of us can testify, at least to some degree, that we have enjoyed the Lord in such a way. This is our partaking of the divine nature, which is constituted with the divine love in essence and with the divine light in expression....Just by contacting God for ten to fifteen minutes...we become a person who is transparent and no longer in darkness or opaqueness. What we should say or do also becomes transparent to us. You may not even have the utterance or know how to explain a matter, yet within you there is the light. You know where you should be, and you know where you are. This is the issue of the partaking of the divine nature.

After having a time with the Lord, you sense that One is within you, living, acting, leading, and guiding you. This One is the divine person, who is the Spirit, and this Spirit is also one of the constituents of the divine nature. Everyone who has been genuinely regenerated has had this kind of experience at least once or twice. You touch the source of grace, which is the divine love, and the source of reality, which is the divine light, in your fellowship with the Lord, and both of these sources are the constituents of the divine nature for your enjoyment. (*God's New Testament Economy*, pp. 321-323)

Further Reading: The Seven Mysteries in the First Epistle of John, ch. 1; *God's New Testament Economy*, chs. 30-32

Enlightenment and inspiration: _____

_____

_____

_____

Hymns, #841

1   Thou art all my life, Lord,
     In me Thou dost live;
   With Thee all God's fulness
     Thou to me dost give.
   By Thy holy nature
     I am sanctified,
   By Thy resurrection,
     Vict'ry is supplied.

2   Now Thy flowing life, Lord,
     Doth enlighten me,
   Bringing in the spirit
     Fellowship with Thee;
   All my need supplying,
     Making Thy demand,
   Leading me to cleansing
     And in Thee to stand.

3   Thy anointing Spirit
     Me shall permeate,
   All my soul and spirit
     Thou wouldst saturate;
   Every part transforming
     Till conformed to Thee,
   Till Thy life shall bring me
     To maturity.

4   Lord, Thy life abundant,
     Flowing, rich and free,
   Constantly refreshes
     And empowers me.
   Death by life is swallowed,
     Weakness is made strong,
   All my bonds are broken,
     Gloom is turned to song.

5   I would give myself, Lord,
     Fully unto Thee,
   That Thy heart's desire
     Be fulfilled in me.
   I no more would struggle
     To myself reform,
   Thus in me to hinder
     What Thou wouldst perform.

6   I would cease completely
       From my efforts vain,
     Let Thy life transform me,
       Full release to gain;
     Build me up with others
       Till in us Thou see
     Thy complete expression
       Glorifying Thee.

Composition for prophecy with main point and sub-points: _____

_____
_____
_____
_____
_____
_____
_____
_____
_____
_____
_____
_____
_____
_____
_____
_____
_____
_____
_____
_____
_____
_____
_____
_____
_____
_____
_____
_____

The Divine Birth and the Children of God

Scripture Reading: 1 John 2:29; 3:1-2, 9; 4:7; 5:1, 4, 18

Day 1   I. **The writings of John on the mysteries of the divine life emphasize the divine birth, which is our regeneration (John 1:12-13; 3:3, 5-6; 1 John 2:29; 3:9; 4:7; 5:1, 4, 18):**

A. The divine birth is the basis of our Christian life (John 3:3, 5; 1 Pet. 1:3, 23).

B. The divine birth, which brings in the divine life, is the basic factor of all the mysteries of the divine life (1 John 1:1-2).

C. The Father is the source of the divine life, the One of whom we have been born with this life (3:1).

D. The divine birth—regeneration—enlivens us with God's life and brings us into a relationship of life, an organic union, with God (Rom. 8:16; 1 Cor. 6:17).

E. To be regenerated simply means to receive the divine life in addition to our human life; through the divine birth eternal life has come into us (John 3:15-16; 1 John 2:25; 5:11-13).

Day 2   F. Regeneration causes us to become a new creation, something which has the element of God within it (Gal. 6:15):

1. Through the divine birth we have the divine life and the divine element, thereby becoming a new creation (2 Cor. 5:17).

2. When we were born again, God's life in Christ entered into us; this life, with the divine element, has been mingled with our spirit to become the new man within us (Eph. 4:24; Col. 3:10).

G. To be regenerated is to receive the tree of life (Gen. 2:9; Rev. 22:2, 14):

1. When we received the Lord Jesus, we received the life of the tree of life (John 11:25; 15:1).

2. We have passed out of the death of the tree of the knowledge of good and evil into the life of the tree of life (5:24; 1 John 3:14).

Day 3   H. To be regenerated is to be born of the Spirit in our spirit (John 3:6, 8):

1. Regeneration takes place in the realm of the human spirit by the Spirit of God with the divine life (vv. 6, 15-16):

   a. The divine birth has taken place organically in our spirit (v. 6).
   b. In regeneration, God in Christ as the life-giving Spirit comes into our spirit to regenerate us with His life and nature (1 Cor. 15:45b; 6:17).
   c. The divine Spirit regenerates the human spirit with the divine life (Rom. 8:2, 10, 16).

2. That which is born of the Spirit of God is our regenerated spirit (John 3:6).

3. In 1 John 5:4 *everything* refers to every person who has been begotten of God; such an expression should refer especially to the part that has been regenerated with the divine life—the spirit of the regenerated believer.

I. In Christ's resurrection He imparted the divine life into us and made us the same as He is in life and nature; this is the basic factor of our regeneration (1 Pet. 1:3; John 3:15-16).

Day 4 **II. By the mysterious divine birth with the divine life, we have become children of God (1:12-13; 1 John 3:1):**

A. It is the greatest wonder in the universe that human beings could be begotten of God and sinners could be made children of God (2:29—3:1; 4:7; 5:1, 4, 18).

B. God's purpose in creating man was not simply to have a sinless man but to have a God-man, one who has the life and nature of God for the corporate expression of God (Gen. 2:9; John 10:10b; 2 Pet. 1:4).

C. The expression *children of God* in 1 John 3:1 is very rich in its implications; it implies that God has been born into us and that we possess His life and nature:

1. To be a child of God means that God has been conceived within us.

2. When we were born of God in our spirit, we were mingled with Him (1 Cor. 6:17).

Day 5

D. By being regenerated, we have become children of God (John 1:12-13; 3:3, 5-6; 1 John 2:29—3:1):

1. We have been begotten of the Father to be children of God (v. 1).

2. For human beings to become children of God is for them to be born of God to have the divine life and nature (John 1:12-13; 3:15-16; 2 Pet. 1:4).

3. Since to be regenerated is to be born of God and to obtain God's life, regeneration automatically causes us to become children of God (John 3:6; Rom. 8:16).

4. The life we receive through regeneration enables us to be and is our authority to be God's children (John 1:12-13).

5. As the children of God with the life and nature of God, we can live God and be the same as God in life, nature, and expression, thus fulfilling the purpose of God's creation of man (Gen. 1:26).

Day 6

E. The children of God have been regenerated of God the Spirit to be God-men, belonging to the species of God to see and enter into the kingdom of God (John 3:3, 5-6):

1. God has a good pleasure to make us, His children, the same as He is in life and nature but not in the Godhead (Eph. 1:5, 9; 5:1).

2. Because we have been born of God, we are the same as God in life and nature but not in the Godhead (Rom. 8:2, 10, 16; 2 Pet. 1:4).

    3. All the children of God are in the divine realm of the divine species.

    4. We should never forget that, as children of God, we are God-men, born of God and belonging to the species of God (John 1:12-13; 3:3, 5).

F. The children of God have a great future with a splendid blessing (1 John 3:2):

    1. The children of God will be like Him in the maturity of life when He is manifested (vv. 1-2).

    2. The right of the God-men to participate in God's divinity includes the right to bear God's likeness (2 Cor. 3:18; Rom. 8:29).

    3. By seeing Him, we will reflect His likeness; this will cause us to be as He is (1 John 3:2).

    4. To partake of the divine nature is already a great blessing and enjoyment, yet to be like God, bearing His likeness, will be a greater blessing and enjoyment (Rev. 4:2-3; 21:11).

Morning Nourishment

John 1:12-13	**But as many as received Him, to them He gave the authority to become children of God, to those who believe into His name, who were begotten not of blood, nor of the will of the flesh, nor of the will of man, but of God.**
1 John 5:1	**Everyone who believes that Jesus is the Christ has been begotten of God, and everyone who loves Him who has begotten loves him also who has been begotten of Him.**

Now we come to what I call the mystery of the divine birth. All those who have been redeemed have had two births: the first, human or natural, and the second, divine. The last verse of [1 John 2] says, "...everyone who practices righteousness also has been begotten of Him." Here the matter of the divine birth is brought in. Then in chapter three, the first verse is, "Behold what manner of love the Father has given to us, that we should be called children of God." From here to the end of chapter five, this thought of divine birth is mentioned repeatedly, and the phrase "born of God" occurs a number of times (3:9; 4:7; 5:1, 4a, 18). (*The Seven Mysteries in the First Epistle of John,* p. 52)

Today's Reading

It is surely a mystery to say that we have been born of God! That we have been created by God is commonly admitted. But to say that God is our Father and that we therefore have His life and nature, is to make a great claim. Do we really believe that we have been born of God? Is God really our Father, not our adopted father or our father-in-law, but the One who has given us His life? Yes, these verses clearly declare that we have been born of God. (*The Seven Mysteries in the First Epistle of John,* p. 52)

First Peter 1:3 says, "Blessed be the God and Father of our Lord Jesus Christ, who according to His great mercy has regenerated us unto a living hope through the resurrection of Jesus Christ from the dead." Regeneration, like redemption and justification, is an aspect of God's full salvation. Redemption and justification solve our problem with God and reconcile us to God. Regeneration enlivens us with God's life and brings us into a relationship of life, an organic union, with God. Hence, regeneration issues and results in a living hope. Such regeneration takes place through the resurrection of Christ from among the dead. When Christ was resurrected, we, His believers, were all included in Him. Thus, we were resurrected with Him (Eph. 2:6). In His resurrection the divine life was imparted to us and made us the same as Christ in life and nature. This is the basic factor of our regeneration.

To be regenerated is to receive another life, God's divine life, in addition to our human life. Through regeneration God imparts His divine life into us. We all have been born of His divine life. This is to be regenerated by God. (*The Conclusion of the New Testament*, p. 201)

Regeneration is not any kind of outward improvement or cultivation; neither is it only a mere change or conversion without life. Regeneration is a rebirth which brings in a new life. It is absolutely a matter of life, not a matter of doing....We have already received the human life from our parents; now we need to receive the divine life from God. Hence, regeneration means to have the divine life of God in addition to the human life which we already possess. Therefore, regeneration requires another birth in order to possess another life. To be regenerated, to be born again, does not mean to adjust or correct ourselves. It means to have the life of God, just as to be born of our parents means to have the life of our parents. To be regenerated is to be born of God (John 1:13), and to be born of God is to have the life of God, that is, the eternal life (3:15-16). If we have the life of God, we are the sons of God. The life of God gives us the right to become the sons of God (John 1:12), because by this life we have the divine nature of God (2 Pet. 1:4) and have the life relationship with God, that is, the sonship (Rom. 8:15; Gal. 4:5-6; [what some versions render as] "adoption" in Greek is "sonship"). (*Life-study of John*, p. 98)

Further Reading: Life-study of John, msg. 8; *Practical Lessons on the Experience of Life,* chs. 1-2*

Enlightenment and inspiration: _____

_____

_____

Morning Nourishment

2 Cor. So then if anyone is in Christ, *he is* a new creation.
5:17 The old things have passed away; behold, they have
become new.

Col. And have put on the new man, which is being renewed
3:10 unto full knowledge according to the image of Him
who created him.

John Truly, truly, I say to you, He who hears My word and
5:24 believes Him who sent Me has eternal life, and does
not come into judgment but has passed out of death
into life.

The believers have been made a new creation by being regenerated. Regeneration causes us to become a new creation, something which has the element of God within it. The old creation has
nothing of the divine element in it. That is why it is old and decay-
ing. Originally, we did not have God's element; therefore, we were
the old creation. It was not until God's element was added into us
that we became a new creation. This is what regeneration has
accomplished in us. Regeneration causes us to have God's life and
His very element, thereby making us a new creation. This new
creation is a marvelous mystery, for it is the mingling of God and
man. As the most wonderful thing in the universe, the new creation has both the human and divine elements. By regeneration
God's element was added into us, and we became a new creation.
(*The Conclusion of the New Testament,* pp. 1403-1404)

Today's Reading

Since we are made a new creation by being regenerated, we
need a clear and accurate understanding of regeneration. To be
regenerated simply means to receive the divine life in addition to
our human life. God's eternal purpose is for man to be a vessel
to contain the divine life. Our being with our human life is a vessel to contain God as life. God's goal is that we receive the divine
life as our real life. This is the meaning of regeneration.

Regeneration of the Spirit is the beginning of the new man
within us. All our experiences of spiritual life are matters of the

new man, who begins within us at the time of our regeneration. Before we were regenerated, we were in Adam, a fallen sinner, an old man. Once we were regenerated, God's life in Christ entered into us. This life is a new element, and when it mingles with our spirit, it becomes the new man within us. (*The Conclusion of the New Testament,* pp. 1404, 1409)

Even if Adam had not fallen, he still would have needed regeneration. That was why God put him in front of the tree of life. If Adam had partaken of the tree of life, he would have been regenerated....We all have a human life. The problem is not a matter of whether or not our human life is good or bad. Regardless of the kind of human life we have, as long as we do not have the divine life, we need to be regenerated....God's eternal purpose is that man be a vessel to contain the divine life. Our being with our human life is a vessel to contain God as life....The divine life is God Himself. God's goal is that we, as people with a human life, receive the divine life into our being as our real life. This is the true meaning of regeneration. Many Christians are not clear about this fact, thinking that...we need to be regenerated because our life is bad and cannot be improved. This concept is wrong. I say once again that even if Adam in the garden of Eden had never fallen, he still would have needed to be regenerated, to be born again, that he might have another life, the life of God. Therefore, to be regenerated is to receive the divine life, God Himself.

Due to human culture and Jewish religion, Nicodemus thought that man needed to behave. Since man must have good conduct and worship God in a proper way, man needs much teaching....Nicodemus was seeking for teachings which belong to the tree of knowledge, but the Lord's answer turned him to the need of life, which belongs to the tree of life (cf. Gen. 2:9-17). The Lord told Nicodemus very emphatically that what he needed was to be born again. (*Life-study of John,* pp. 97-99)

Further Reading: The Conclusion of the New Testament, msg. 129; *The God-man Living,* msg. 1

Enlightenment and inspiration: _____

_____

_____

_____

Morning Nourishment

John   That which is born of the flesh is flesh, and that which
3:6   is born of the Spirit is spirit.
1 John   For everything that has been begotten of God over-
5:4   comes the world; and this is the victory which has
       overcome the world—our faith.
1 Pet.   Blessed be the God and Father of our Lord Jesus
1:3   Christ, who according to His great mercy has regen-
       erated us unto a living hope through the resurrection
       of Jesus Christ from the dead.

To be born anew is to be born of the Spirit in our spirit. The
divine Spirit regenerates our human spirit with God's divine life.
Regeneration, that is, receiving the divine life, is absolutely a
matter that transpires in our spirit. Our spirit was made by God
for this very purpose. We have such a special organ, our human
spirit, deep within us. In His creation, God made us with a spirit
for the purpose that one day we might exercise it to contact Him
and to receive Him into our being. The function of the human
spirit is to contact God. Regeneration is not a matter of our mind,
emotion, or will; it is altogether a matter in our spirit. (*Life-study
of John*, pp. 103-104)

Today's Reading

[We are born of God] in our spirit. That which is born of the
Spirit is spirit. God is a Spirit, and only a spirit can touch a Spirit.
Only a spirit can be born of a Spirit. So, regeneration is absolutely
a matter in our spirit. It does not matter whether you have a sober
mind, a proper emotion, or a strong will. Such things are in
another realm. Regeneration transpires in the realm of our spirit.
Our spirit is the sphere in which regeneration transpires. In order
to be regenerated, you do not exercise your mind, will, or emotion.
Simply open yourself up, forgetting what you are, and from deep
within your spirit, call on the name of the Lord Jesus, believing in
Him. If you do this, immediately,...God the Spirit will enter into
your spirit and you will be regenerated....When you say, "Lord
Jesus, I believe in You," you are reborn in your spirit.

In John 3:6, the Lord said, "That which is born of the flesh is flesh, and that which is born of the Spirit is spirit." Regeneration is not a birth of the flesh that brings forth flesh. Regeneration is a birth of the Spirit, God's Spirit, that brings forth spirit, our regenerated spirit. Flesh is our natural man, our old man, our outward man, born of our parents who are flesh. But spirit, our regenerated spirit, is our spiritual man, our new man, our inward, or inner man (2 Cor. 4:16; Eph. 3:16), born of God who is the Spirit....Now our spirit is a regenerated spirit and becomes our new being....To be regenerated is to have the divine eternal life as the new source and the new element of our new being. (*Life-study of John,* pp. 104-105)

First Peter 1:3 reveals that our regeneration took place "through the resurrection of Jesus Christ from the dead." It is crucial for us to realize that we were regenerated when Christ was resurrected. This means that, in the sight of God, we were regenerated before we were born, since Christ's resurrection was our regeneration. Before we became part of the old creation through our natural birth, we were already a part of the new creation through Christ's resurrection. Thus, our regeneration was accomplished once for all more than nineteen centuries ago. In our experience we may have been reborn some years ago, but from the divine perspective our regeneration was fully accomplished when Christ was resurrected. Our experience of regeneration is based fully upon the fact that it has already been accomplished through the resurrection of Christ.

When Christ was resurrected, we, His believers, were all included in Him. Thus, we were resurrected with Him (Eph. 2:6). In His resurrection Christ imparted the divine life into us and made us the same as He is in life and in nature. This is the basic factor of our regeneration. (*The Conclusion of the New Testament,* pp. 1406-1407)

Further Reading: Life-study of John, msg. 9; *The Knowledge of Life,* chs. 3-4

Enlightenment and inspiration: _____

_____

_____

_____

Morning Nourishment

1 John
3:1

Behold what manner of love the Father has given to us, that we should be called children of God...

4:7

Beloved, let us love one another, because love is of God, and everyone who loves has been begotten of God and knows God.

Phil.
2:15

That you may be blameless and guileless, children of God without blemish in the midst of a crooked and perverted generation, among whom you shine as luminaries in the world.

The believers have been reborn to be the children of God. "As many as received Him, to them He gave the authority to become children of God, to those who believe into His name, who were begotten not of blood, nor of the will of the flesh, nor of the will of man, but of God" (John 1:12-13). To be regenerated is to be born of God, and to be born of God is to have the life of God, that is, the eternal life. If we have the life of God, we are the children of God, for the life of God gives us the authority, the right, to become the children of God, because by this life we have the nature of God and a life relationship with Him. Since regeneration means to be born of God, it automatically causes us to become the children of God. Now we are God's children, and He is our Father. (*The Conclusion of the New Testament*, p. 1413)

Today's Reading

We have been begotten of the Father, the source of life, to be the children of God. It is the greatest wonder in the universe that human beings can be begotten of God and that sinners can be made children of God. Through regeneration...we have received the divine life, the eternal life. This life...enables us to be His children. Now the Spirit witnesses with our spirit that we are children of God (Rom. 8:16). Even at times when we are weak or backsliding we still have the deep conviction that we are children of God, for once we have been born of God we are His children forever.

Regeneration involves an eternal birth relationship that cannot be dissolved. No birth can be reversed. No one can become unborn once he is born. Just as this is a fixed principle in physical life, it is even more solid and substantial in the spiritual realm. Once we are born of God, we are eternally His children, regardless of our condition. Though we may turn away from the Lord temporarily, the birth relationship can by no means be terminated. This great fact gives us much confidence and boldness in the face of failure and sin. No failure can terminate the birth relationship we have with God.

In Philippians 2:15 Paul speaks of the believers as children of God. This implies regeneration, the new birth. To be a child of God means that we have been born of God, that God has been conceived within us. When we became children of God, God was conceived in our being. This means that when we were born of God in our spirit, we were mingled with Him. God has been conceived within us, and we have been born of Him to become His children.

The expression "children of God" in 2:15 is very rich in its implications. It implies that God has actually been born into us and that we possess His life and nature. Sometimes we may say, "I am just a sinner saved by grace." Although this, of course, is true, it is very shallow compared with the revelation in the New Testament. If we know the truth of the Word, we shall not say that we are merely sinners saved by grace. We shall have the boldness to declare, "I am a child of God born of the Spirit!" No doubt, we are sinners who have been saved by God's grace. But because we have been born of God, we are now His children. How marvelous!

We can be children of God only by having the life of God. How wonderful it is to have God's life! Just as a child has the life of his parents, so as children of God we have the life of God. All those who are truly children of God need to realize that they have the divine life within them. (*The Conclusion of the New Testament,* pp. 1413-1414, 1217)

Further Reading: The Conclusion of the New Testament, msg. 100; *Life-study of Philippians,* msg. 13; *Incarnation, Inclusion, and Intensification,* ch. 4

Enlightenment and inspiration: _____

_____

_____

_____

Morning Nourishment

1 John 2:29—3:1	If you know that He is righteous, you know that everyone who practices righteousness also has been begotten of Him. Behold what manner of love the Father has given to us, that we should be called children of God; and we are....
Rom. 8:16	The Spirit Himself witnesses with our spirit that we are children of God.
Gen. 1:26	...God said, Let Us make man in Our image, according to Our likeness; and let them have dominion over the fish of the sea and over the birds of heaven and over the cattle and over all the earth and over every creeping thing that creeps upon the earth.

In 1 John 3:1 John refers to the divine birth and to the begetting Father. Of the Triune God implied in 2:29, the Father is particularly mentioned. He is the source of the divine life, the One of whom we have been born with this life. The love of God is manifested by sending His Son to die for us so that we may have His life and thus become His children (4:9; John 3:16; 1:12-13). The sending of His Son is for begetting us. Hence, the love of God is a begetting love, particularly in the Father. (*Life-study of 1 John,* p. 224)

Today's Reading

The word "children" in First John 3:1 corresponds to "begotten of Him" in 2:29. We have been begotten of the Father, the source of life, to be the children of God, the Owner of the children. We partake of the Father's life to express the Triune God.

In 3:1 John says, "Because of this the world does not know us, because it did not know Him." The Greek word rendered "because" may also be translated on this account or for this reason. For the reason that we are the children of God by a mysterious birth with the divine life, the world does not know us. The world is ignorant of our regeneration by God; it does not know us, because it did not know God Himself. It was ignorant of God, so it is also ignorant of our divine birth. (*Life-study of 1 John,* pp. 224-225)

When we receive God's eternal life, we receive all that God is in Himself and all that is in God, and we have God's nature and the capabilities and function in God Himself. Hence, we can be as God is and do what God does, that is, we can be like God and live God out.

By being regenerated we have become the children of God (John 1:12-13). Since to be regenerated is to be born of God and to obtain God's life, regeneration automatically causes us to become the children of God, bringing us into a relationship with God in life and nature. The life we receive from God through regeneration enables us to become the children of God, and this life is also our authority to be His children. As God's children, who have God's life and nature, we can be like God, live God, and express God, thus fulfilling the purpose of God's creation of man. (*Truth Lessons—Level One,* vol. 4, p. 53)

The Spirit witnesses with our spirit that we who once were children of the devil are now the children of God (Rom. 8:16). Even at times when we are weak or backsliding we still have the deep conviction that we are children of God, for once we have been born of God we are His children forever.

John 1:12 and 13 say, "As many as received Him, to them He gave the authority to become children of God, to those who believe into His name, who were begotten not of blood, nor of the will of the flesh, nor of the will of man, but of God." Here we see that the children of God have been begotten of God, not of blood, nor of the will of the flesh, nor of the will of man. "Blood" here signifies the physical life; the will of the flesh denotes the will of fallen man after man became flesh; and the will of man refers to the will of man created by God. When we became children of God, we were not born of our physical life, our fallen life, or our created life—we were born of God, the uncreated life. For human beings to become children of God is for them to be born of God to have the divine life and nature. (*The Conclusion of the New Testament,* p. 1072)

Further Reading: Life-study of 1 John, msg. 26; *Truth Lessons— Level One,* lsn. 41

Enlightenment and inspiration: _____

_____
_____
_____

Morning Nourishment

John 3:5 Jesus answered,...Unless one is born of water and the Spirit, he cannot enter into the kingdom of God.

1 John 3:2 Beloved, now we are children of God, and it has not yet been manifested what we will be. We know that if He is manifested, we will be like Him because we will see Him even as He is.

Rom. 8:29 Because those whom He foreknew, He also predestinated *to be* conformed to the image of His Son, that He might be the Firstborn among many brothers.

If we are not born anew, we do not have the capacity to see the kingdom of God [John 3:3]. To be born anew is to be born of water, signifying the death of Christ, and of the Spirit, signifying Christ's resurrection. We need to die with Christ and be resurrected to be a new person of another, new species, new kind.

The kingdom of God is the reign of God. This divine reign is a realm, not only of the divine dominion but also of the divine species, in which are all the divine things.

God became flesh to enter into the human species, and man becomes God in His life and nature, but not in His divine Godhead, to enter into His divine species. In John 3 the kingdom of God refers more to the species of God than to the reign of God. (*Crystallization-study of the Gospel of John*, pp. 122-123)

Today's Reading

The believers, who are born of God by regeneration to be His children in His life and nature but not in His Godhead (John 1:12-13), are more in God's kind than Adam was. Adam had only the outward appearance of God without the inward reality, the divine life. We have the reality of the divine life within us and we are being transformed and conformed to the Lord's image in our entire being. It is logical to say that all the children of God are in the divine realm of the divine species.

Thus, in regeneration God begets gods. Man begets man. Goats beget goats....If the children of God are not in God's kind, in God's species, in what kind are they? If they are not gods, what are they? We all who are born of God are gods. But for utterance, due to the theological misunderstanding, it is better to say that we are God-men in the divine species, that is, in the kingdom of God. (*Crystallization-study of the Gospel of John,* pp. 123-124)

[According to 1 John 3:2], since we are the children of God, we shall be like Him in the maturity of life when He is manifested. To be like Him is "what we will be." This has not yet been manifested. This indicates that the children of God have a great future with a more splendid blessing. We shall not only have the divine nature, but shall also bear the divine likeness. To partake of the divine nature is already a great blessing and enjoyment; yet to be like God, bearing His likeness, will be a greater blessing and enjoyment.

The pronoun "He" in 3:2 refers to God and denotes Christ, who is to be manifested. This not only indicates that Christ is God, but also implies the Divine Trinity. When Christ is manifested, the Triune God will be manifested. When we see Him, we shall see the Triune God; and when we are like Him, we shall be like the Triune God.

In verse 2 John says, "We will be like Him because we will see Him even as He is." This means that by seeing Him we shall reflect His likeness (2 Cor. 3:18). This will cause us to be as He is.

Verse 2 indicates that the children of God have a great future. However, I have heard some saints say that they do not have a future. These saints need to realize that they have a great future with splendid blessings. Our future is indicated by the word "it has not yet been manifested what we will be." What we will be is a divine mystery. Because it is such a mystery, it must be something great. We are not able to imagine what our future will be. The fact that our future has not yet been manifested indicates that it will be wonderful. Although it has not been manifested what we will be, we know that when the Son is manifested, we will be like the Triune God. (*Life-study of 1 John,* pp. 225-226)

Further Reading: Crystallization-study of the Gospel of John, msg. 12;
   Basic Lessons on Life, lsn. 8; *Life Lessons,* lsn. 42

Enlightenment and inspiration: _____

_____

_____

_____

Hymns, #30

1   What love Thou hast bestowed on us,
     We thank Thee from our heart;
   Our Father, we would worship Thee
     And praise for all Thou art.

2   Thy heart Thou hast revealed to us,
     Made known th' eternal will;
   Within the Son Thou hast come forth,
     Thy purpose to fulfill.

3   Thou gavest Thy beloved Son
     In love to come and die,
   That we may be Thy many sons,
     As heirs with Him, made nigh.

4   Through Him we have Thy very life
     And Thou our Father art;
   Thy very nature, all Thyself,
     Thou dost to us impart.

5   Thy Spirit into ours has come
     That we may "Abba" cry;
   Of Spirit born, with Spirit sealed,
     To be transformed thereby.

6   The many sons to glory brought
     Is Thine eternal goal,
   And to Thy Son's own image wrought,
     Thou wilt conform the whole.

7   Throughout Thy transformation work
     Thou dost direct each one,
   From glory unto glory bring
     Until the work is done.

8   What love Thou, Father, hast bestowed;
     We'll ever grateful be;
   We'll worship Thee forevermore
     And praise unceasingly.

Composition for prophecy with main point and sub-points: _____

_____

_____

_____

_____

_____

_____

_____

_____

_____

_____

_____

_____

_____

_____

_____

_____

_____

_____

_____

_____

_____

_____

_____

_____

_____

_____

_____

_____

_____

_____

_____

_____

_____

_____

_____

_____

_____

_____

Our Spirit Born of God with the Seed of God
for Us to Grow with the Growth of God
for the Building of God

Scripture Reading: 1 John 3:9; 5:4a, 18; Mark 4:26; 1 Pet. 1:23; Col. 2:19; 1 Cor. 3:9

Day 1

I. The intrinsic element of the entire teaching of God's eternal economy is that the Triune God in humanity, the wonderful Christ as the Spirit of the glorified Jesus, is sown into God's chosen people as the seed of life, the seed of God, so that He might grow in them, live in them, develop in them, and be expressed from within them as the farm of God for the building up of the church as the house of God and the kingdom of God (Mark 4:11-20, 26-29; Matt. 16:18; 1 Cor. 3:9; 1 Pet. 1:23; cf. Deut. 22:9).

II. Regeneration means that the seed of the divine, uncreated, eternal, and unlimited life with the divine nature has been sown into our spirit; through regeneration our spirit has been born of God, and the seed of God abides in it (Mark 4:26; 1 Pet. 1:23; 1 John 3:9; 5:11-12; 2 Pet. 1:4):

A. "That which is born of the flesh is flesh, and that which is born of the Spirit is spirit" (John 3:6):

1. "Flesh" is our natural man, our old man, our outer man, born of our parents who are flesh; but "spirit," our regenerated spirit, is our spiritual man, our new man, our inner man, born of God who is the Spirit (2 Cor. 4:16; Eph. 3:16).

2. The divine Spirit regenerates our human spirit with God's divine life, thus making our spirit life (Rom. 8:10).

3. Regeneration brings forth in us a newborn spirit, a new spirit (Ezek. 36:26), indwelt by

and mingled with God's divine Spirit to be
one spirit (Rom. 8:16; 1 Cor. 6:17).

Day 2
&
Day 3

B. "Everything that has been begotten of God overcomes the world" (1 John 5:4a):

1. The word *everything* refers especially to our
   regenerated spirit, our spirit of faith; our regenerated spirit overcomes the world, and our
   regenerated spirit with the seed of God in it
   does not practice sin (2 Cor. 4:13; 1 John 3:9).

2. Our regenerated spirit keeps us from living
   in sin, and when we are in our regenerated
   spirit, the evil one does not touch us (5:18;
   cf. Psa. 91:1-2).

3. When we are in our spirit where the pneumatic Christ dwells, we are in Christ, the
   One in whom Satan, the ruler of the world,
   has nothing (no ground, no chance, no hope,
   and no possibility in anything) (2 Tim. 4:22;
   John 14:30b; cf. Phil. 4:13).

4. The whole world lies in the evil one; the
   only exception to this is our regenerated
   spirit (1 John 5:19).

5. Only one thing in the whole universe does
   not have Satan's footprints on it—our
   regenerated spirit; as long as we remain
   in our regenerated spirit, we will be kept
   absolutely in the dispensing Triune God,
   and Satan will have no way in us (cf. John
   17:11, 15; Num. 6:24).

C. There is only one true God, and this true God is
in our spirit; whatever is not in the spirit or of
the spirit is an idol, something that is against
Christ or that replaces Christ (1 John 5:19-21):

1. Anything we do that is not in the regenerated spirit and that does not live out the
   Lord Spirit is an idol; an idol is anything
   within us that we love more than the Lord
   and that replaces the Lord in our life
   (cf. Ezek. 14:3).

Day 4
    2. We need to flee into the presence of God in our spirit in order to be kept from the evil one and to guard ourselves from idols; we must flee into our spirit to directly touch God and be face to face with God for the growth of His seed in us (Heb. 6:18-20; Exo. 33:11a, 14; 2 Cor. 2:10).

III. **The seed of the divine life, the seed of God, that has been sown into us needs to grow in us so that we may grow with the growth of God, with the increase of God as life, and be transformed in life to become precious materials for God's building in life (Col. 2:19; 1 Cor. 3:6, 9, 12a):**

  A. According to the Bible, growth equals building; this takes place by the growth of Christ as the divine seed of life within us; the way to grow is composed of four main items (Eph. 4:15-16):

    1. We must love the Lord; in order to grow, we must go to the Lord to pray definitely and purposely that He will grant us a love for Him (1 John 4:19; 2 Cor. 5:14; Matt. 22:37; John 14:23; 1 Cor. 2:9).

Day 5
    2. We must deal with the Lord thoroughly by confessing all our failures, shortcomings, weaknesses, filthiness, and trespasses in the light of His presence so that we may have a good and pure conscience (1 John 1:7, 9; 1 Tim. 1:5; 2 Tim. 1:3; Acts 24:16).

    3. We must learn how to discern our spirit and exercise our spirit (Heb. 4:12; Eph. 3:16; 2 Tim. 1:6-7; Rom. 8:6).

    4. We must always stay in contact with the Lord, remaining in touch with Him (1 John 1:3).

Day 6
  B. After being sown into our spirit, the divine seed needs to grow in the soil of our heart, and this growth needs our cooperation (Matt. 13:3-9, 19-23):

    1. For the growth of Christ as the life seed in us, we must deal with the Lord daily to be

poor in spirit, to be emptied in our spirit,
acknowledging that we have nothing, know
nothing, can do nothing, and are nothing
apart from Christ as the Spirit, the new,
present, and "now" Christ (5:3).

2. For the growth of Christ as the life seed in
   us, we must deal with the Lord daily to be
   pure in heart, keeping our heart with all
   vigilance; God wants our heart to be soft,
   pure, loving, and at peace so that He can
   have a free way to grow in us (v. 8; Prov.
   4:23; Matt. 13:19-23).

3. For the growth of Christ as the life seed in
   us, we must drink the guileless milk and
   eat the solid food of the word of God (1 Pet.
   2:2; Heb. 5:12-14).

4. For the growth of Christ as the life seed in
   us, we must enjoy the watering of the Spirit
   by the gifted members of the Body (1 Cor.
   3:6, 9).

5. When Christ as the seed of life grows in us
   and fully makes His home in our hearts, we
   will be filled unto all the fullness of God—
   the Body of Christ as the corporate expression of the Triune God (Eph. 3:17, 19b).

Morning Nourishment

John   Jesus answered and said to him,...Unless one is born
3:3   anew, he cannot see the kingdom of God.
   6   That which is born of the flesh is flesh, and that
      which is born of the Spirit is spirit.
Mark   And He said, So is the kingdom of God: as if a man
4:26-27   cast seed on the earth, and sleeps and rises night and
      day, and the seed sprouts and lengthens...

In Mark 4:26-29 we have the parable of the seed....The kingdom of God is the reality of the church brought forth by the resurrection life of Christ through the gospel (1 Cor. 4:15). Regeneration is its entrance (John 3:5), and the growth of the divine life within the believers is its development (2 Pet. 1:3-11).

The man in Mark 4:26 is the sower in verse 3. This sower is the Slave-Savior, who was the Son of God coming to sow Himself as the seed of life in His word (v. 14) into men's hearts so that He might grow and live in them and be expressed from within them.

The seed in verse 26 is the seed of the divine life (1 John 3:9; 1 Pet. 1:23) sown into the believers of the Slave-Savior. The casting of the seed here indicates that the kingdom of God...[and] the church in this age (Rom. 14:17) are [matters] of life, the life of God, which sprouts, grows, bears fruit, matures, and produces a harvest.

Mark 4:28 says, "The earth bears fruit by itself: first a blade, then an ear, then full grain in the ear." The earth here is the good earth (v. 8) and signifies the good heart created by God (Gen. 1:31) for His divine life to grow in man. Such a good heart works together with the seed of the divine life sown into us to grow and bear fruit spontaneously for the expression of God. (*Life-study of Mark*, pp. 139-140)

Today's Reading

[John 3:6 shows that] regeneration is not a birth of the flesh that brings forth flesh. Regeneration is a birth of the Spirit, God's Spirit, that brings forth spirit, our regenerated spirit. Flesh is our natural man, our old man, our outward man, born of our parents who are flesh. But spirit, our regenerated spirit, is our spiritual

said again, "Go home!" Eventually, you had to say, "Forget about this!" Thus, you went home. Who kept you? Who brought you back home? It was the regenerated spirit within you that kept you. We are all vile sinners and are all capable of committing gross sins, yet all these years we have been kept. This is because our regenerated spirit has kept us. Within us we have something that has been regenerated, something that has been begotten of God. This something is our spirit.

What is within this spirit? God Himself is in it. First John 3:9 says that it is God's seed, that is, God Himself and Christ Himself. This is a very mysterious matter. In our regenerated spirit is God Himself and Christ Himself as our seed. All we need to do is to abide in our regenerated spirit and to live and walk in our spirit. First John tells us that we have something that has been regenerated. We have God's seed in our regenerated spirit. Thus, we need to abide in our regenerated spirit. If we do, then we are of God.

First John also tells us that the whole world lies in the evil one (5:19)....In God's eyes the whole world, that is, all human beings, all human societies, and all things, are under the hand of Satan. The only exception is our regenerated spirit. We should not think that the unbelievers are under the authority of Satan and that we are not. We cannot speak in such a general way. It is possible that our mind is still under Satan's authority and that only our regenerated spirit is not. Actually, it is very possible that even our reading of the Word and our prayer are under Satan's authority, because they may come not out of our regenerated spirit but out of our mind, emotion, and preference. I hope that we would be under a finer, deeper light. Only one thing in the whole universe and on the whole earth does not have Satan's footprints on it—our regenerated spirit. Aside from our regenerated spirit, all the other parts of our being are under the hand of Satan. (*Living in the Spirit,* pp. 59-60)

Further Reading: Life-study of 1 John, msg. 39; *Life-study of Numbers,* pp. 80-81

Enlightenment and inspiration: _____

_____

_____

_____

Morning Nourishment

1 John 5:20-21   **And we know that the Son of God has come and has given us an understanding that we might know Him who is true; and we are in Him who is true, in His Son Jesus Christ. This is the true God and eternal life. Little children, guard yourselves from idols.**

We must ask ourselves whether the Lord is in our prayer, our reading of the Bible, and our bread-breaking meeting. If we are not in the spirit and no one else is in the spirit, then the Lord is not in these things, and all these things are still under Satan's hand. Not only our dancing, going to nightclubs, and playing mah-jongg are under Satan's hand, but even our reading of the Word, our prayer, and our going to meetings can be under Satan's hand unless they are done in the spirit. This is because the only thing in the whole universe that does not have Satan in it is our regenerated spirit. Unless we are in our spirit, whatever we do is under Satan's hand.

Where is God today? He is right in our spirit. We must see that our spirit is God's Holy of Holies. The three parts of our being—our spirit, our soul, and our body—correspond exactly to the three parts of the tabernacle. Our spirit is the Holy of Holies, and God's habitation in the heavens is also the Holy of Holies. According to Hebrews, these two realms are connected. God's habitation, the place where God dwells, is the Holy of Holies. Today our spirit is also the Holy of Holies. Our spirit as the Holy of Holies is connected and joined to the Holy of Holies in the heavens. If this were not so, we would not be able to enter the Holy of Holies and touch the throne of grace for timely help, as mentioned in Hebrews 4:16.... Our spirit today is the Holy of Holies. (*Living in the Spirit*, pp. 61-62)

Today's Reading

The church is not in a physical building. The church is in our spirit. The church is God's Holy of Holies because the church is the aggregate of the regenerated spirits of all the saints.

Therefore, when we pray, read the Word, worship, and serve, we must be in our spirit and in the church, because the church is the aggregate of our spirits. Sometimes we are not in the spirit, yet we come together to worship. At such a time, we must realize that our worship is not the worship in the church. If we are in such a situation, we are no longer inside the Holy of Holies but outside. Only our regenerated spirit as the Holy of Holies is not under the authority of Satan....In this entire universe God has drawn a line around one thing—our spirit....God has set a limit for Satan, saying, "Satan, this is off limits to you! Do not transgress this boundary!"

Finally, there is a warning: "Little children, guard yourselves from idols" (1 John 5:21). This means that anything that is not of the true God, not of the eternal life, and not in the regenerated spirit is an idol. Our reading of the Bible may be an idol, our prayer may be an idol, and even our bread-breaking may be an idol, because we may be reading the Word, praying, worshipping, serving, and even breaking bread outside of our regenerated spirit! We may be lying in the evil one because we are not in the spirit.

You may say that there are no idols in your meeting hall. However, you may not realize that your idols are your selves, your scheming, and your domineering. You may not realize that your desire to win others over so that they will agree with you is an idol. You may not realize that your idol is your insistence on teaching others the spiritual experience you had three years ago. You may love your Bible and insist that others read it the same way you do. This is also an idol. Whatever is not in the spirit is an idol. Whatever is not of the spirit is an idol.

Anything we do that is not in the regenerated spirit and that does not live out the Lord Spirit is an idol. Today there is only one true God, and this true God is in only one place, that is, our spirit. Everything outside of this spirit is an idol. If our bread-breaking and our praising are not in the spirit, they are false. Our bearing of responsibilities and our work may also be false if they are not in the spirit. Our insistence with one another in our service is also an idol. (*Living in the Spirit*, pp. 62-65)

Further Reading: Living in the Spirit, ch. 5

Enlightenment and inspiration: _____

_____

_____

_____

Morning Nourishment

Heb. ...We who have fled for refuge to lay hold of the hope
6:18-20   set before *us*, which we have as an anchor of the soul,
both secure and firm and which enters within the
veil, where the Forerunner, Jesus, has entered for us...
Matt.   ..."You shall love the Lord your God with all your
22:37   heart and with all your soul and with all your mind."

Hebrews 4 says that the word of God is living and able to
pierce through us, dividing our spirit, as the Holy of Holies, from
the soul that surrounds it (v. 12). Hebrews 6 says that we are all
fleeing (v. 18). From what are we fleeing? We are fleeing from our
idols, our flesh, our ideas, our views, our dissenting thoughts, and
our old experiences....The Greek word translated *fled* implies "to
flee intensively, seriously, and speedily," just as Lot...fled from
Sodom. This is what the writer of the book of Hebrews meant. He
seemed to be saying, "O Hebrew brothers, you need to flee! Flee
from Judaism and your old doctrines."

Then where should we flee to? We should flee to the Holy of
Holies. We should flee from our disposition, our views among the
co-workers, and our dissenting thoughts. If we do not flee, we will
be under the hand of the devil. Our Forerunner has already
entered into the spirit, into the Holy of Holies. Today we should not
remain in the outer court or in the Holy Place. We all need to flee
to the Holy of Holies, to the presence of God. We must flee until we
have nothing else to flee from, until we are directly touching God
and are face to face with God. (*Living in the Spirit,* pp. 65-66)

Today's Reading

According to the Bible, growth equals building. The Lord
Jesus declared, "I will build My church" (Matt. 16:18). This building takes place by the growth of the divine seed within us.

The Triune God, the source of life, has sown Himself in Christ
as a seed into our being. Once this seed comes into us, it meets
something within us—our spiritual nutrients—and it begins to
grow. The degree of growth depends not on the divine seed but on
how many nutrients we afford this seed. Matthew 13 indicates

that only the good soil (vv. 8, 23) affords the adequate nutrients for the growth of the divine seed. (*Life-study of 1 & 2 Samuel,* p. 197)

From the New Testament teaching and revelation, the way to grow is comprised of four main items. If we practice these, then not only are we in life but we are on the way of growth, and we also will know how to help others to grow.

If we spend time to study [Matthew 13], we can see that the lack of growth is due to one thing: After a person is saved by the divine seed sown into him, he may not love the Lord. If we study our history and compare it with the New Testament, we will find that the first step, the first main thing needed, for a believer to grow is to love the Lord. If we do not have a love for the Lord, we are superficial; our heart is either stony or things other than the Lord Himself choke the seed in it. We need a love for the Lord.

If we simply pray, "Lord, be merciful to me. Grant me a love for You," our stony heart will be dealt with. It will be dug and made deep. There will be a digging within not by anything else, but by love. In order to grow, we must go to the Lord to pray definitely and purposely that He will grant us a love for Him....This love will do much work to get rid of all the stones within us...[and deliver] us from all the choking elements. The more we try, exercise, and endeavor by ourselves to overcome all the things that choke, the more we will be defeated. The only thing that can deliver us from any kind of choking is love. Therefore, we must learn to pray that the Lord would grant us such a love.

This is absolutely different from any religion....[The Lord Jesus] asks us to believe in Him and to love Him. We must have faith in Him, and we must have love toward Him....Then we will see that we are starting to grow. When we start to love the Lord, we start to grow. There is no other way. The only way for Christians to begin growing is by firstly knowing how to love the Lord. (*Practical Lessons on the Experience of Life,* pp. 199-201)

Further Reading: The Crucial Revelation of Life in the Scriptures, ch. 10; *The Tree of Life,* ch. 13

Enlightenment and inspiration: _____

_____

_____

_____

Morning Nourishment

1 John
1:9
If we confess our sins, He is faithful and righteous to forgive us our sins and cleanse us from all unrighteousness.

Heb.
4:12
For the word of God is living and operative and sharper than any two-edged sword, and piercing even to the dividing of soul and spirit and of joints and marrow, and able to discern the thoughts and intentions of the heart.

The second main item we must have is confession, or clearance. After we begin to love the Lord, we must have a clear dealing with ourselves in order to have the real growth in life....In other words, we must deal with our conscience....We need a pure conscience, and one who has a pure conscience is one who has thoroughly confessed all the sinful things, dirtiness, failures, and trespasses. We must go to the Lord to have such a dealing. Sometimes we need three days for this. I do not believe you can finish your confession within only one or two hours. If we mean business with the Lord, we will need a longer time to have a thorough dealing. This is not something legal; it is a principle.

Why are many Christians not spiritually healthy? It is simply because their conscience is not purged. Within their conscience are many accusations and offenses. Some even realize this, but they are not willing to make a confession, so to one degree or another they are frustrated....If we are not willing to confess, it is because we do not love the Lord....Perhaps at this time you do not feel that you are wrong in anything, but when you start to love the Lord, you will realize how wrong you are in many things, with people and with the Lord. You will sense the need to confess to the Lord. (*Practical Lessons on the Experience of Life*, pp. 202-203)

Today's Reading

After we have love and a pure conscience, we must learn the lesson of always exercising our spirit. To be soulish is easier than to be sinful. It is not easy for you to induce me to be sinful, but it may be very easy to induce me to be soulish. For many seeking

Christians it is not easy to be sinful,…but it is very easy to be soulish, to say things in the soul, to do things in the soul, to contact people in the soul, and to deal with things in the soul. If we do not exercise the spirit, we are merely in the soul.

If we are about to argue with someone and we say to ourselves, "I must try not to argue with people," that will not work. The more we try not to argue, the more we will argue.…We should forget about arguing and learn to always exercise our spirit. When we exercise our spirit, all the arguments are gone. The only way for us to be delivered from arguing, or from anything in the soul, is to forget about the soul, forget about all things related to the soul, and learn to exercise the spirit. Then when we meet a brother, we will not need to tell ourselves not to argue; we will know only to exercise our spirit to contact the Lord. Then we will have the growth.

To know the spirit in this way is to be strengthened into the inner man [Eph. 3:16].…The inner man, that is, the spirit, needs to be strengthened. We all have to learn to exercise the spirit. All weaknesses, problems, confusions, and disturbances come from the soul. There is no need to deal with all these things. Simply forget about the soul and learn to exercise the spirit. Then all the problems will be resolved.…If we practice this, there will be the real growth.

We also must always stay in contact with the Lord. Any time we are not in contact with the Lord, we are in degradation, not in growth.

From my own learning and experiences, I have come to realize that the simplest way for Christians to grow is the above four matters: love the Lord, deal with Him thoroughly, learn to exercise the spirit, and keep in contact with Him. If we do these things, we will see the growth. (*Practical Lessons on the Experience of Life,* pp. 205-207)

Further Reading: Practical Lessons on the Experience of Life, ch. 16; *The Spirit with Our Spirit,* ch. 8; *The God-man Living,* msg. 10

Enlightenment and inspiration: _____

_____

_____

_____

Morning Nourishment

1 Pet. **As newborn babes, long for the guileless milk of the**
2:2 **word in order that by it you may grow unto salvation.**

The intrinsic growth of the church is through the feeding on the guileless milk and the solid food of the word by the members of Christ (1 Pet. 2:2; Heb. 5:12-14).

As members of the Body of Christ, we should drink the guileless milk of the word that we may grow. Then we must eat the solid food of the word so that we may grow even more. Our eating of the word causes us to grow in a strong way. The Word is full of food, but some only get knowledge according to the letter when they read the Bible. This is a shame because…Christ is our real food and every page of the Bible is a description of this rich Christ. He is either expressed or implied throughout the whole Bible.… When we come to the Bible, we should come with a heart seeking after Christ. We should pray, "Lord, I come to Your Word. I do not care for teachings alone, but I care for You. Lord, feed me with Yourself through this Word." We all should have such a prayer.

Christ, as the life-giving Spirit, is food to us (John 6:57; 1 Cor. 15:45b). As the life-giving Spirit, He is dispensing Himself into us and supplying us with Himself as life.

When we open any page of the Bible, we should read with a seeking heart and pray, "Lord, I love You, so I come to Your Word. Be my drink and be my food." When we pray in this way, we will realize that Christ, who is now the life-giving Spirit, is within us dispensing Himself and supplying us with Himself as our food. This supply of life will cause us to grow. (*The Organic Building Up of the Church as the Body of Christ to Be the Organism of the Processed and Dispensing Triune God*, pp. 22, 26)

Today's Reading

The church grows through eating, and also through the watering on the Body of Christ by its gifted members (1 Cor. 3:6). We believers are living plants who have been planted into Christ (1 Cor. 3:6a, 9b). Christ is our good ground, our earth. He is the rich soil into which we have been planted and in which we grow. Once a plant has been planted, it needs to be watered....Paul said, "I planted, Apollos watered" (1 Cor. 3:6a). For our spiritual growth, we need the food that the Word provides, and we also need the watering that the gifted ones provide.

If you are in the meetings of the church, you will be blessed with much watering. Regardless of how much time you spend reading the Bible in your home, it cannot replace the meetings of the church....You may say that you do not like the meetings, but whether you like the meetings or not, the "sprinklers" are there "sprinkling."...The gifted members of the Body of Christ, the servants of God, are like the sprinklers on the lawns; they have the ability to sprinkle us with water. The more they talk to us about the Bible, the more they sprinkle us with water. We can testify that when we come to a ministry meeting and listen to the speaking of the gifted persons with all the Bible verses, we can never be the same. Whether or not we understand everything, we always go away from such meetings with the water of the Bible.

The intrinsic growth of the church is through the giving of growth in life to the members of Christ by God (1 Cor. 3:6c). The gifted ones may do the planting and the watering, but it is God who gives the growth in life.

We need the feeding from the Bible directly, and we need the watering from the ones who know the Bible more. God goes along with our reading of the Word and with the speaking of the gifted members to give us the growth. The feeding and the watering are the top means used by Him to give His life to us. When we get into the Word, we are feeding. When we get under the speaking of the word, we receive the watering. Then God gives the growth. (*The Organic Building Up of the Church as the Body of Christ to Be the Organism of the Processed and Dispensing Triune God*, pp. 27-29)

Further Reading: The Organic Building Up of the Church as the Body of Christ to Be the Organism of the Processed and Dispensing Triune God, ch. 2; The Advance of the Lord's Recovery Today, ch. 4; The Knowledge of Life, ch. 10

Enlightenment and inspiration: _____

_____

_____

_____

Hymns, #1132

1   Lord, teach us how to pray,
    Not as the nations do in vain,
    But turn us from our way,
    And cause us, Lord, to call on You each day—
        Lord Jesus, grow in us.

2   Lord, You're the seed of life;
    You've sown Yourself into our heart,
    And now You have a start;
    So day by day more life to us impart—
        Lord Jesus, grow in us.

3   Lord Jesus, soften us;
    You know the source from which we came.
    By calling on Your name,
    Lord, let no earth unturned nor rocks remain—
        Lord Jesus, grow in us.

4   Lord, how Your light makes clear
    That we could not but e'er fail You;
    Yet there's a message true,
    The seed of life within us will break through—
        Lord Jesus, grow in us.

5   Make us in spirit poor;
    Lord, take whate'er we think we know.
    We'll open to life's flow,
    And thus take in the life that makes us grow—
        Lord Jesus, grow in us.

6   Lord, make us pure in heart;
    For we'll be not content until
    You all our being fill,
    O Lord, renew our mind, emotion, will—
        Lord Jesus, grow in us.

7   Yes, Lord, impress our heart
    That we must take You in each day;
    The seed will have its way;
    Your growing brings the kingdom here to stay—
        Lord Jesus, grow in us.

8   Amen!—The growth in life!
    There's nothing that Your life can't do;
    Our every part renew.
    We'll make it, we'll make it just by You.
        Lord Jesus, grow in us.
        Lord Jesus, grow in us.

Composition for prophecy with main point and sub-points: _____

_____
_____
_____
_____
_____
_____
_____
_____
_____
_____
_____
_____
_____
_____
_____
_____
_____
_____
_____
_____
_____
_____
_____
_____
_____
_____
_____
_____
_____
_____
_____
_____
_____
_____
_____

*The Divine Light, the Divine Truth,
and the Divine Reality*

Scripture Reading: 1 John 1:5-7; 5:6; 2 John 1-2, 4; 3 John 1,
3-4, 8

Day 1   I. **The divine light is the nature of God's
expression, it shines in the divine life, and it
is the source of the divine truth (1 John 1:5-6;
John 1:4; 8:12):**

A. Light is God's shining, God's expression; when
God is expressed, the nature of that expression
is light (1 John 1:5):

1. To walk in the divine light is to live, move,
act, and have our being in the divine light,
which is God Himself (v. 7).

2. The shining of the divine light makes old
things new (2:7-8).

3. If we are under God's dispensing, we participate in God's nature as light and are constituted with this element of His nature
(1:5; 2 Cor. 4:6).

Day 2   B. The divine light shines in the divine life (John
1:4; 8:12):

1. A great principle in the Bible is that light
and life go together (Psa. 36:9).

2. Where light is, there is life, and where life
is, there is light (John 1:4).

C. The divine light is the source of the divine truth
(vv. 5, 9; 18:37):

1. When the divine light shines upon us, it
becomes the truth, which is the divine reality (8:12, 32).

2. When the divine light shines, the divine
things become real to us.

3. Because light is the source of truth, and
truth is the issue of light, when we walk
in the light, we practice the truth (1 John
1:6-7).

D. The divine light, which shines in the divine life and issues in the divine truth, is embodied in the Lord Jesus, God incarnate (John 1:1, 4, 14; 8:12; 9:5; 14:6).

Day 3   II. **The truth concerning the person of Christ is the basic and central element of John's mending ministry (1 John 4:2-3, 15; 2 John 7-9).**

III. **In John's writings the Greek word for *truth* (*aletheia*) denotes all the realities of the divine economy as the content of the divine revelation, conveyed and disclosed by the holy Word (John 17:17; 18:37):**

A. Truth is God, who is light and love, incarnated to be the reality of the divine things for our possession (1:1, 4, 14-17).

B. Truth is Christ, who is God incarnated and in whom all the fullness of the Godhead dwells bodily, as the reality of God and man, of all the types, figures, and shadows of the Old Testament, and of all the divine and spiritual things (Col. 2:9, 16-17; John 4:23-24).

C. Truth is the Spirit, who is Christ transfigured, as the reality of Christ and of the divine revelation (14:16-17; 15:26; 16:13-15).

D. Truth is the Word of God as the divine revelation, which reveals and conveys the reality of God and Christ and of all the divine and spiritual things (17:17).

E. Truth is the contents of the faith (belief), which are the substantial elements of what we believe, as the reality of the full gospel (Eph. 1:13; Col. 1:5).

F. Truth is the reality concerning God, the universe, man, man's relationship with God and with his fellow man, and man's obligation to God, as revealed through creation and the Scriptures (Rom. 1:18-20; 2:2, 8, 20).

G. Truth is the genuineness, truthfulness, sincerity, honesty, trustworthiness, and faithfulness

of God as a divine virtue and of man as a human
virtue, and as an issue of the divine reality (3:7;
15:8; 2 Cor. 11:10; 1 John 3:18).

H. Truth denotes things that are true or real, the
true or real state of affairs (facts), reality, veracity, as the opposite of falsehood, deception, dis-
simulation, hypocrisy, and error (Mark 12:32;
John 16:7; Acts 26:25; Rom. 1:25).

Day 4 **IV. *Your truth* (3 John 3, lit.) is the truth concerning Christ, especially His deity, by the
revelation of which the recipient's way of
life is determined and to which the recipient
holds as his fundamental belief:**

A. The objective truth becomes ours; thus, the
truth becomes subjective to us in our daily walk
(2 John 2).

B. Our life is determined, shaped, and molded by
the revelation of this truth; this means that we
live, walk, and behave in the divine reality, the
Triune God, who is our enjoyment (v. 4).

**V. To walk in the truth is to live in the truth; the
truth concerning the person of Christ
should be not only our belief but also our
living, a living that testifies to our belief
(2 John 4; 3 John 3-4).**

Day 5 **VI. To be fellow workers in the truth is to join
ourselves to those who, as faithful workers
of the truth, work for God in the divine
truth, and it is to do whatever we can to support these traveling brothers and promote
this work (vv. 5-8).**

**VII. It is crucial that we see the picture of the
divine reality presented by John in his Epistles (1 John 5:6; 3 John 12):**

A. The central factor in 1 John is the divine reality—the Triune God dispensed into us for our
experience and enjoyment (4:13-14; 5:6).

B. The divine reality is the divine person—the
Father, the Son, and the Spirit—becoming our

experience, enjoyment, and constituent through incarnation, human living, crucifixion, resurrection, and ascension (John 1:14, 29; 20:22).

C. The divine reality is the Father in the Son and the Son as the Spirit dispensed into God's chosen, redeemed, and regenerated people so that they may enjoy Him as life, the life supply, and everything (14:6, 12-13, 16-20).

Day 6 **VIII. Truthfulness is the revealed divine reality— the Triune God dispensed into man in the Son, Jesus Christ—becoming man's genuineness and sincerity, that man may live a life that corresponds with the divine light and worship God, as God seeks, according to what He is (2 John 1; 3 John 1; John 3:19-21; 4:23-24):**

A. This is the virtue of God becoming our virtue, by which we love the believers (Rom. 3:7; 15:8; 1 John 3:18).

B. In such genuineness the apostle John, who lived in the divine reality of the Trinity, loved the one to whom he wrote (2 John 1; 3 John 1).

C. To worship the Father in truthfulness is to worship Him with the Christ who has saturated our being to become our personal reality through our experience and enjoyment of the Triune God as the divine reality (John 4:23-24).

Morning Nourishment

1 John ...God is light and in Him is no darkness at all.
1:5, 7 ...But if we walk in the light as He is in the light,
we have fellowship with one another, and the blood
of Jesus His Son cleanses us from every sin.
2 Cor. ...The God who said, Out of darkness light shall
4:6 shine, is the One who shined in our hearts to illuminate the knowledge of the glory of God in the
face of Jesus Christ.

The divine light is the essence of God's expression. When God
is expressed, the essence of that expression is light. What is the
divine truth? The divine truth is the issue of the divine light. When
the divine light shines in us, it becomes the divine truth, which is
the divine reality. This means that when the divine light shines in
us, we receive the divine reality. We may also say that the divine
light brings us the divine reality. (*Life-study of 1 John,* p. 75)

Today's Reading

In 1 John 1:5 John says, "And this is the message which we
have heard from Him and announce to you, that God is light and
in Him is no darkness at all." In verse 7 he speaks a further word
concerning light: "But if we walk in the light as He is in the light,
we have fellowship with one another, and the blood of Jesus His
Son cleanses us from every sin." As we have indicated, the divine
light is the nature, the essence, of God's expression and the source
of the divine truth. This divine light shines in the divine life. Hence,
if we do not have the divine life, we cannot have the divine light.

John 1:4 says, "In Him was life, and the life was the light of
men." In Christ there is the divine life, and this life is the divine
light. Therefore, life is light. When we have the divine life, we also
have the divine light. (*Life-study of 1 John,* pp. 75-76)

According to His New Testament economy, God is now dispensing Himself into us. Surely what God dispenses into us is what He
is in His nature. When God is dispensed into us, His nature is also
dispensed into us. For God to dispense Himself into us means that
He is dispensing Himself into us with what He is in His nature.

We have seen that God's nature includes Spirit as the nature of God's person, love as the nature of God's essence, and light as the nature of God's expression. Since God is dispensing Himself in His nature into us, the more we are under God's dispensing, the more we have of His Spirit, love, and light.

When we are under God's dispensing, our living will not only be with Spirit and love, but also with light. Our natural love is in darkness. Only one kind of love is full of light, and that is the love that comes from God's dispensing. If we are under God's dispensing day by day, we shall behave with Spirit, with love, and with light. With how much Spirit, love, and light do you behave in your daily life? This is a test of whether or not you are under God's dispensing....[God] has a nature which is Spirit, love, and light. If we are under the dispensing of such a God, certainly He will infuse us with His nature, that is, with Himself as Spirit, the nature of His person, love, the nature of His essence inwardly, and light, the nature of His expression outwardly.

If we are one with Him and if we are daily under His dispensing, we shall be those who spontaneously live a life that is full of Spirit, love, and light.

We need to consider all the aspects of what God is in His person. Although God's person has many aspects, in nature He is very simple: He is Spirit, love, and light. If we are under His dispensing, our reactions will indicate to others that we have much Spirit, love, and light, even that we are constituted of Spirit, love, and light.

If we are under God's dispensing, surely we shall participate in God's nature as Spirit, love, and light. Then we shall become those who are living in Spirit, love, and light in the sense that we have been constituted of these elements of God's nature. In our living there will be no need for us to perform, to act deliberately. Rather, we shall simply live a life according to the divine nature. (*The Conclusion of the New Testament*, pp. 69-71)

Further Reading: The Conclusion of the New Testament, msg. 7; *Life-study of 1 John*, msg. 17

Enlightenment and inspiration: _____

_____

_____

_____

Morning Nourishment

John ...Jesus spoke to them, saying, I am the light of the
8:12 world; he who follows Me shall by no means walk
    in darkness, but shall have the light of life.
  32 And you shall know the truth, and the truth shall
    set you free.
Psa. For with You is the fountain of life; / In Your light
36:9 we see light.

There is a line in the whole Bible which continuously speaks of
life and light together. Where light is, there is life. This is a great
principle in the Bible. Psalm 36:9 says, "With You is the fountain
of *life;* in Your *light* we see light." This also clearly speaks of the
relationship between life and light. Life always follows light, and
only light can bring forth life. (*The Knowledge of Life,* pp. 204-205)

Today's Reading

Truth is the expression of light, just as grace is the expression
of love. Whenever light shines, we receive truth. Light shines in
darkness. In 1 and 2 Timothy, two books dealing with degradation,
truth is mentioned often because during a period of darkness there
is the need for the shining of the light, the expression of the light.

Truth is the shining of light. Wherever there is light, there is
God, for God is light (1 John 1:5). When the light shines upon us, it
becomes the truth. In Romans 8 Paul encourages us to walk
according to the spirit, but in John's second and third Epistles,
also written in a time of degradation, John speaks of walking in
the truth. Although in his other writings John emphasized life, in
these two Epistles he spoke much about the truth. For example,
in 3 John 4 he says, "I have no greater joy than these things, that I
hear that my children are walking in the truth." Whenever we are
in a time of degradation and darkness, we need the shining of the
light so that we may know how to walk in the proper way. (*Truth
Messages,* pp. 8-9)

To walk in the divine light is not merely to dwell in this light; it
is to live, move, act, do things, and have our being in the divine
light, the light which is actually God Himself. When we dwell,

live, and have our being in God, we walk in the divine light, which is the expression of God.

When the divine light shines, we see all the different truths, and these truths are realities. But when we do not have the divine light but are rather in darkness, we have the sense that everything is vanity and emptiness. I would ask you to consider your experience. When you are in the divine light, you can see the truth, the reality. For example, when you are in the light, God is a reality to you, and the divine life is also a reality. Furthermore, God's holiness, love, and grace are all realities to you. When we walk in the light, we see one reality after another. However, when we are in darkness, nothing is real to us. On the contrary, everything is empty, vain. When we are in darkness, we do not have any reality because we do not see anything. Instead of the sense of reality, we have the sense of emptiness and vanity.

When we dwell in God, we are in the fellowship. When we are in this fellowship, we are in light. Then as we walk in the light, Christ, the Spirit, the church, the Body, and the members of the Body are all real to us. We may testify and say, "Praise the Lord that I see Christ, the Spirit, the church, the Body, and the ground of the church! How wonderful! All this is real to me."

We have seen that the divine light is the nature of God's expression, that it is the source of the divine truth, and that it shines in the divine life. Now we must go on to see that the divine light is embodied in Jesus as God incarnate. Because He is the embodiment of the divine light, the Lord Jesus said, "I am the light of the world; he who follows Me shall by no means walk in darkness, but shall have the light of life" (John 8:12). He spoke a similar word in John 9:5: "While I am in the world, I am the light of the world." The divine light that issues in truth and shines in life is embodied in the Person of the Lord Jesus, who is God incarnate. This matter is deep and profound. (*Life-study of 1 John*, pp. 62, 77)

Further Reading: The Knowledge of Life, ch. 14; *Truth Messages*, msgs. 1-2

Enlightenment and inspiration: _____

_____

_____

_____

Morning Nourishment

John
15:26 ...When the Comforter comes, whom I will send to you from the Father, the Spirit of reality, who proceeds from the Father, He will testify concerning Me.
16:13 But when He, the Spirit of reality, comes, He will guide you into all the reality; for He will not speak from Himself, but what He hears He will speak; and He will declare to you the things that are coming.
17:17 Sanctify them in the truth; Your word is truth.

In 2 John 4 through 6 John speaks concerning the walk in truth and love. Verse 4 says, "I rejoiced greatly that I have found some of your children walking in truth, even as we received commandment from the Father." The truth concerning the Person of Christ is the basic and central element of John's mending ministry. When he found the children of the faithful believer walking in truth, he rejoiced greatly (3 John 3-4).

In verse 4 John uses the word "walking." As in 1 John 1:7, where John speaks of walking in the light, the word "walk" means to live, behave, and have our being. The truth concerning the Person of Christ should not only be our belief; it should also be our living. (*Life-study of 2 John*, p. 5)

Today's Reading

The Greek word *aletheia* means truth or reality (versus vanity), verity, veracity, genuineness, sincerity. It is John's highly individual terminology, and it is one of the profound words in the New Testament. This word denotes all the realities of the divine economy as the content of the divine revelation, contained, conveyed, and disclosed by the holy Word.

According to the New Testament, truth is first God, who is light and love, incarnated to be the reality of the divine things—including the divine life, the divine nature, the divine power, the divine glory—for our possession, so that we may enjoy Him as grace, as revealed in John's Gospel (John 1:1, 4, 14-17)....Second, truth in the New Testament denotes Christ, who is God incarnated and in whom all the fullness of the Godhead dwells bodily

(Col. 2:9), to be the reality of: a) God and man (John 1:18, 51; 1 Tim. 2:5); b) all the types, figures, and shadows of the Old Testament (Col. 2:16-17; John 4:23-24); and c) all the divine and spiritual things....Third, truth is the Spirit, who is Christ transfigured (1 Cor. 15:45b; 2 Cor. 3:17), the reality of Christ (John 14:16-17; 15:26) and of the divine revelation (John 16:13-15). Hence, the Spirit is the reality (1 John 5:6).

Truth is also the Word of God as the divine revelation, which not only reveals but also conveys the reality of God and Christ and of all the divine and spiritual things. Hence, the Word of God also is reality (John 17:17).

According to the New Testament, truth is also the contents of the faith (belief), which is the substantial elements of what we believe as the reality of the full gospel (Eph. 1:13; Col. 1:5).

In the Bible truth is also the reality concerning God, the universe, man, man's relationship with God and with one another, and man's obligation to God, as revealed through creation and the Scripture (Rom. 1:18-20; 2:2, 8, 20).

[Truth] also denotes the genuineness, truthfulness, sincerity, honesty, trustworthiness, and faithfulness of God as a divine virtue (Rom. 3:7; 15:8), and of man as a human virtue (Mark 12:14; 2 Cor. 11:10; Phil. 1:18; 1 John 3:18) and as an issue of the divine reality (John 4:23-24; 2 John 1; 3 John 1).

In the New Testament truth is not only the Triune God, the Word of God, the contents of the faith, and the reality concerning God, man, and the universe. Truth is also the genuineness, truthfulness, sincerity, honesty, trustworthiness, and faithfulness of God as a divine virtue and of man as a human virtue and as an issue of the divine reality. According to this understanding of truth, this divine virtue first belongs to God, and then through our experience of Christ this virtue also becomes ours. After the divine virtue is experienced by us, it becomes our virtue, a virtue that is an issue of the divine reality. (*Life-study of 1 John,* pp. 79, 81-82, 90)

Further Reading: Life-study of 1 John, msgs. 9-11

Enlightenment and inspiration: _____

_____

_____

_____

Morning Nourishment

2 John 2	For the sake of the truth which abides in us and will be with us forever.
3 John 3-4	For I rejoiced greatly at the brothers' coming and testifying to your *steadfastness in the* truth, even as you walk in truth. I have no greater joy than these things, that I hear that my children are walking in the truth.

In 2 John 1 and 2 the apostle John speaks of loving in truthfulness, of knowing the truth, of the truth abiding in us, and of the truth being with us forever. In his third Epistle he…speaks…especially of walking in the truth, saying that he has "no greater joy than these things, that I hear that my children are walking in the truth" (3 John 4). The emphasis on the truth in these Epistles indicates that they were written during a time of degradation when many had gone astray from the truth. (*Truth Messages,* pp. 12-13)

Today's Reading

In 3 John 3, John speaks of "your steadfastness in the truth," which translated literally is "your truth." "Your truth" is the truth concerning Christ, especially His deity, by the revelation of which the recipient's way of life is determined and to which the recipient holds as his fundamental belief. The thought here is deep. John's thought is that the objective truth becomes ours. Hence, the truth becomes subjective to us in our daily walk. This truth is the reality of Christ's deity. Our life is determined and shaped by the revelation of this truth. This means that we live, walk, and behave in the divine reality of the Triune God, who is our enjoyment. This enjoyment shapes our walk, our way of life. This indicates that our way of life is determined, shaped, molded by what we believe concerning the Person of Christ and by what we have seen and enjoyed of this reality. This truth is actually the Triune God becoming our enjoyment.

We believe that the Triune God became a man and lived on earth, died on the cross for our redemption, and in resurrection became a life-giving Spirit. Now this life-giving Spirit is the consummation of the Triune God. This Spirit is the consummation of all that the Father is and of all that the Son is as a person possessing divinity and humanity. Christ the Son is the very God and also a real man, who has accomplished redemption and is now the Life-giver, the life-imparting Spirit. We believe this, and this belief now shapes, determines, molds, our way of life. This is what it means to walk in truth.

The philosophy a person holds will determine his way of life. What a person believes will always shape his living. We Christians walk in the divine truth. This means that our way of life is determined, shaped, molded, by the divine reality—the Triune God Himself—which we enjoy.

In verse 3 John says to Gaius, "Even as you walk in truth." The one who receives this word not only holds to the truth, but also walks and lives in the truth. The truth concerning the Person of Christ should not only be our belief, but should also be our living, a living that testifies to our belief. The truth in which we walk, therefore, becomes our truth in our daily life.

In verse 4 John continues, "I have no greater joy than these things, that I hear that my children are walking in the truth." As in 2 John 4, "truth" here is the divine reality, especially concerning the Person of Christ as revealed in John's Gospel and first Epistle, that is, that Christ is both God and man, having both deity and humanity, possessing both the divine nature and the human nature, to express God in human life and to accomplish redemption with divine power in human flesh for fallen human beings so that He may impart the divine life into them and bring them into an organic union with God. The second and third Epistles of John emphasize this truth. The second warns the faithful believers against receiving those who do not abide in this truth, and the third encourages the believers to receive and help those who work for it. (*Life-study of 3 John*, pp. 3-5)

Further Reading: Life-study of 2 John, msg. 1; *Life-study of 3 John*, msg. 1

Enlightenment and inspiration: _____

_____

_____

_____

Morning Nourishment

3 John
7-8 For on behalf of the Name they went out, taking nothing from the Gentiles. We therefore ought to support such ones that we may become fellow workers in the truth.

1 John
5:6 This is He who came through water and blood, Jesus Christ; not in the water only, but in the water and in the blood; and the Spirit is He who testifies, because the Spirit is the reality.

Both 2 John and 3 John are based on 1 John. Both 2 and 3 John indicate that we need to live in truth and walk in truth. The difference is that in 2 John there is the prohibition of participating in heresy, of participating in any teaching that is against this truth. We must stay away from any teaching or any person who is against the reality of the Triune God. But in 3 John there is the encouragement to help the fellow workers in the truth. We need to join ourselves to anyone who works for the divine reality of the Triune God that we are enjoying, and we need to do whatever we can to promote this work. Hence, in 2 John there is a negative attitude toward heresy and in 3 John, a positive attitude toward the work for the truth. Whether our attitude should be negative or positive depends on whether the particular situation is for the divine reality or against it. (*Life-study of 3 John*, p. 5)

Today's Reading

The concern of the apostle John in writing his three Epistles was the enjoyment of the Triune God. This is also our concern today. Among believers there is a great lack of the divine reality and hardly any enjoyment of the Triune God. Instead,...Christians have religion with doctrines, creeds, rituals, and practices.... As a whole, today's religion is a "vanity fair."...Instead of reality and the enjoyment of the Triune God, with religion there is all manner of vanity. We, however, need to be careful not to merely talk about truth, reality, without having the genuine experience.

What is the truth, the divine reality, that John talks about in his Epistles? This reality is the Father in the Son and the Son as the Spirit dispensed into God's chosen, redeemed, and regenerated people so that they may enjoy Him as life, life supply, and everything in the new creation life. Actually, this truth, this reality, is the enjoyment of the Triune God. The Father in the Son became a man, who died on the cross to accomplish redemption and resurrected to become the life-giving Spirit. Now He can dispense Himself into His chosen people so that they may have Him for their enjoyment and also as their life, life supply, and everything they need for the life of the new creation. This is the divine reality as revealed in the Epistles of John.

It is vital that we all see what the divine reality is. The Divine Trinity should become our subjective enjoyment. This...has been neglected by Christians today. Therefore, in the Lord's recovery we have been charged by the Lord to pay full attention to this matter.

In the recovery we should not have the words "reality" and "truth" as mere terms. If we have only terms, then we are still in the realm of doctrine, although it may be doctrine of a higher standard and more complete truth. We all need to see that the truth, the reality, is the divine Person—the Father, the Son, and the Spirit—becoming our enjoyment and even our constituent.

We all must see the picture of the divine reality presented by John in his Epistles. This is a picture of the Triune God becoming our enjoyment through incarnation, human living, crucifixion, resurrection, and ascension. Whoever is against this enjoyment is a false prophet, a deceiver, an antichrist. But whoever is for the enjoyment of the Triune God is an honest and faithful worker for the truth, and we should be joined to that one and participate in his work. Anything that replaces this divine reality is a substitute for it, is an idol, and we should garrison ourselves against it....If we see this vision, we shall be clear concerning the situation of today's religion, and we shall also be clear concerning our burden in the Lord's recovery. (*Life-study of 3 John*, pp. 5-7, 17)

Further Reading: Life-study of 2 John, msg. 2; Life-study of 3 John, msg. 2

Enlightenment and inspiration: _____

_____

_____

_____

Morning Nourishment

2 John   The elder to the chosen lady and to her children,
1   whom I love in truthfulness, and not only I but also
          all those who know the truth.
John   But an hour is coming, and it is now, when the true
4:23-24   worshippers will worship the Father in spirit and
          truthfulness, for the Father also seeks such to wor-
          ship Him. God is Spirit, and those who worship
          Him must worship in spirit and truthfulness.

In 2 John 1, John speaks of loving in truthfulness. Truthfulness and truth are from the same word in Greek. According to
John's usage of this word, especially in his Gospel, "truthfulness"
in this verse denotes the revealed divine reality—the Triune God
dispensed into man in the Son, Jesus Christ—becoming man's
genuineness and sincerity, that man may live a life that corresponds to the divine light (John 3:19-21) and worship God, as God
seeks, according to what He is (John 4:23-24). This is the virtue of
God (Rom. 3:7; 15:8) becoming our virtue by which we love the
believers. This is the genuineness, truthfulness, sincerity, honesty, trustworthiness, and faithfulness of God as a divine virtue
and of man as a human virtue (Mark 12:14; 2 Cor. 11:10; Phil.
1:18; 1 John 3:18), and as an issue of the divine reality (3 John 1).
In such truthfulness, the apostle John, who lived in the divine
reality of the Trinity, loved the one to whom he wrote. (*Life-study
of 2 John,* p. 2)

Today's Reading

In 1 John 3:17 and 18 John [says], "But whoever has the livelihood of the world and sees that his brother has need and shuts up
his affections from him, how does the love of God abide in him?
Little children, let us not love in word nor in tongue but in deed
and truthfulness." The livelihood of the world in verse 17 refers to
material things, to the necessities of life. In verse 18, *deed* is versus *word,* and *truthfulness* versus *tongue. Tongue* denotes the
play of vain talk. *Truthfulness,* or *truth,* denotes the reality of love.
Truthfulness denotes sincerity, in contrast with *tongue,* as *deed*

with *word*. *Truth* here denotes the genuineness, the sincerity, of God as a divine virtue becoming a human virtue as an issue of the divine reality. Therefore, the truth in this verse is the reality of God becoming our virtue.

John says that we should not love the brothers merely in word or in tongue, not merely telling the saints that we love them. This is not love in truth, love in reality. To love the saints in truth or reality means to love them in the divine reality that becomes our virtue, something that is honest, faithful, sincere, and real. We should love the brothers in this way. Of course, this kind of love in truth includes a love that supplies the needy ones with material things or money when necessary. We should not love the brothers with vain words; we should love them in truth and even with our livelihood.

We should not think that to love in truth is simply to love in the human virtue of sincerity. No, here John is not speaking of the natural human virtue of sincerity. The truth here is more than human sincerity; it is the divine reality becoming our virtue. Thus, it is the expression of what God is. This means that in loving the saints we should express God.

In experiencing Christ we enjoy God the Father, God the Son, and God the Spirit. This enjoyment issues in a reality that we may call our personal reality. This personal reality is a matter of having Christ saturating our inner being. When we have this reality, we have Christ in our spirit, heart, mind, emotion, and will. This is the Christ whom we have experienced becoming our reality. Now we should worship God not only in our spirit, but also worship Him with this reality, which is the Christ we experience in our daily living. This is not only the divine reality for our enjoyment; this is also our human reality, our personal reality, which comes out of our enjoyment of the divine reality. This human reality is the issue of the divine reality which we enjoy daily. This is the proper understanding of reality in John 4:23 and 24. (*Life-study of 1 John*, pp. 247, 86)

Further Reading: Life-study of 1 John, msgs. 28, 18

Enlightenment and inspiration: _____

_____

_____

_____

Hymns, #865

1 In spirit and in truth, O Lord,
     We meet to worship here;
   As taught by Christ, the Son of God,
     We now in Him draw near.

2 Thank God, He is a Spirit true,
     So near, so dear to us;
   That we may contact Him in life,
     In truth to worship thus.

3 A spirit God has made for us
     That we may worship Him,
   Not striving, serving outwardly,
     But seeking from within.

4 Regenerated by the Lord,
     Renewed in mind and heart,
   He dwells within us as our life
     True worship to impart.

5 We worship here according to
     The inner consciousness,
   Anointed by His Spirit now
     His fulness we express.

6 In truth we serve and worship too,
     In shadows nevermore,
   In Christ, the one reality,
     The Father we adore.

7 To God we offer Christ the Lord
     Whom we experience;
   With God we too delight in Him,
     His light and sweetness sense.

8 In spirit and reality
     Together here we meet,
   To worship, praise, and fellowship
     Around the mercy-seat.

Composition for prophecy with main point and sub-points: _____

_____

_____

_____

_____

_____

_____

_____

_____

_____

_____

_____

_____

_____

_____

_____

_____

_____

_____

_____

_____

_____

_____

_____

_____

_____

_____

_____

_____

_____

_____

_____

_____

_____

_____

_____

Reading Schedule for the Recovery Version of the Old Testament with Footnotes

Wk.	Lord's Day	Monday	Tuesday	Wednesday	Thursday	Friday	Saturday
1	☐ Gen 1:1-5	☐ 1:6-23	☐ 1:24-31	☐ 2:1-9	☐ 2:10-25	☐ 3:1-13	☐ 3:14-24
2	☐ 4:1-26	☐ 5:1-32	☐ 6:1-22	☐ 7:1—8:3	☐ 8:4-22	☐ 9:1-29	☐ 10:1-32
3	☐ 11:1-32	☐ 12:1-20	☐ 13:1-18	☐ 14:1-24	☐ 15:1-21	☐ 16:1-16	☐ 17:1-27
4	☐ 18:1-33	☐ 19:1-38	☐ 20:1-18	☐ 21:1-34	☐ 22:1-24	☐ 23:1—24:27	☐ 24:28-67
5	☐ 25:1-34	☐ 26:1-35	☐ 27:1-46	☐ 28:1-22	☐ 29:1-35	☐ 30:1-43	☐ 31:1-55
6	☐ 32:1-32	☐ 33:1—34:31	☐ 35:1-29	☐ 36:1-43	☐ 37:1-36	☐ 38:1—39:23	☐ 40:1—41:13
7	☐ 41:14-57	☐ 42:1-38	☐ 43:1-34	☐ 44:1-34	☐ 45:1-28	☐ 46:1-34	☐ 47:1-31
8	☐ 48:1-22	☐ 49:1-15	☐ 49:16-33	☐ 50:1-26	☐ Exo 1:1-22	☐ 2:1-25	☐ 3:1-22
9	☐ 4:1-31	☐ 5:1-23	☐ 6:1-30	☐ 7:1-25	☐ 8:1-32	☐ 9:1-35	☐ 10:1-29
10	☐ 11:1-10	☐ 12:1-14	☐ 12:15-36	☐ 12:37-51	☐ 13:1-22	☐ 14:1-31	☐ 15:1-27
11	☐ 16:1-36	☐ 17:1-16	☐ 18:1-27	☐ 19:1-25	☐ 20:1-26	☐ 21:1-36	☐ 22:1-31
12	☐ 23:1-33	☐ 24:1-18	☐ 25:1-22	☐ 25:23-40	☐ 26:1-14	☐ 26:15-37	☐ 27:1-21
13	☐ 28:1-21	☐ 28:22-43	☐ 29:1-21	☐ 29:22-46	☐ 30:1-10	☐ 30:11-38	☐ 31:1-17
14	☐ 31:18—32:35	☐ 33:1-23	☐ 34:1-35	☐ 35:1-35	☐ 36:1-38	☐ 37:1-29	☐ 38:1-31
15	☐ 39:1-43	☐ 40:1-38	☐ Lev 1:1-17	☐ 2:1-16	☐ 3:1-17	☐ 4:1-35	☐ 5:1-19
16	☐ 6:1-30	☐ 7:1-38	☐ 8:1-36	☐ 9:1-24	☐ 10:1-20	☐ 11:1-47	☐ 12:1-8
17	☐ 13:1-28	☐ 13:29-59	☐ 14:1-18	☐ 14:19-32	☐ 14:33-57	☐ 15:1-33	☐ 16:1-17
18	☐ 16:18-34	☐ 17:1-16	☐ 18:1-30	☐ 19:1-37	☐ 20:1-27	☐ 21:1-24	☐ 22:1-33
19	☐ 23:1-22	☐ 23:23-44	☐ 24:1-23	☐ 25:1-23	☐ 25:24-55	☐ 26:1-24	☐ 26:25-46
20	☐ 27:1-34	☐ Num 1:1-54	☐ 2:1-34	☐ 3:1-51	☐ 4:1-49	☐ 5:1-31	☐ 6:1-27
21	☐ 7:1-41	☐ 7:42-88	☐ 7:89—8:26	☐ 9:1-23	☐ 10:1-36	☐ 11:1-35	☐ 12:1—13:33
22	☐ 14:1-45	☐ 15:1-41	☐ 16:1-50	☐ 17:1—18:7	☐ 18:8-32	☐ 19:1-22	☐ 20:1-29
23	☐ 21:1-35	☐ 22:1-41	☐ 23:1-30	☐ 24:1-25	☐ 25:1-18	☐ 26:1-65	☐ 27:1-23
24	☐ 28:1-31	☐ 29:1-40	☐ 30:1—31:24	☐ 31:25-54	☐ 32:1-42	☐ 33:1-56	☐ 34:1-29
25	☐ 35:1-34	☐ 36:1-13	☐ Deut 1:1-46	☐ 2:1-37	☐ 3:1-29	☐ 4:1-49	☐ 5:1-33
26	☐ 6:1—7:26	☐ 8:1-20	☐ 9:1-29	☐ 10:1-22	☐ 11:1-32	☐ 12:1-32	☐ 13:1—14:21

Reading Schedule for the Recovery Version of the Old Testament with Footnotes

Wk.	Lord's Day	Monday	Tuesday	Wednesday	Thursday	Friday	Saturday
27	☐ 14:22—15:23	☐ 16:1-22	☐ 17:1—18:8	☐ 18:9—19:21	☐ 20:1—21:17	☐ 21:18—22:30	☐ 23:1-25
28	☐ 24:1-22	☐ 25:1-19	☐ 26:1-19	☐ 27:1-26	☐ 28:1-68	☐ 29:1-29	☐ 30:1—31:29
29	☐ 31:30—32:52	☐ 33:1-29	☐ 34:1-12	☐ Josh 1:1-18	☐ 2:1-24	☐ 3:1-17	☐ 4:1-24
30	☐ 5:1-15	☐ 6:1-27	☐ 7:1-26	☐ 8:1-35	☐ 9:1-27	☐ 10:1-43	☐ 11:1—12:24
31	☐ 13:1-33	☐ 14:1—15:63	☐ 16:1—18:28	☐ 19:1-51	☐ 20:1—21:45	☐ 22:1-34	☐ 23:1—24:33
32	☐ Judg 1:1-36	☐ 2:1-23	☐ 3:1-31	☐ 4:1-24	☐ 5:1-31	☐ 6:1-40	☐ 7:1-25
33	☐ 8:1-35	☐ 9:1-57	☐ 10:1—11:40	☐ 12:1—13:25	☐ 14:1—15:20	☐ 16:1-31	☐ 17:1—18:31
34	☐ 19:1-30	☐ 20:1-48	☐ 21:1-25	☐ Ruth 1:1-22	☐ 2:1-23	☐ 3:1-18	☐ 4:1-22
35	☐ 1 Sam 1:1-28	☐ 2:1-36	☐ 3:1—4:22	☐ 5:1—6:21	☐ 7:1—8:22	☐ 9:1-27	☐ 10:1—11:15
36	☐ 12:1—13:23	☐ 14:1-52	☐ 15:1-35	☐ 16:1-23	☐ 17:1-58	☐ 18:1-30	☐ 19:1-24
37	☐ 20:1-42	☐ 21:1—22:23	☐ 23:1—24:22	☐ 25:1-44	☐ 26:1-25	☐ 27:1—28:25	☐ 29:1—30:31
38	☐ 31:1-13	☐ 2 Sam 1:1-27	☐ 2:1-32	☐ 3:1-39	☐ 4:1—5:25	☐ 6:1-23	☐ 7:1-29
39	☐ 8:1—9:13	☐ 10:1—11:27	☐ 12:1-31	☐ 13:1-39	☐ 14:1-33	☐ 15:1—16:23	☐ 17:1—18:33
40	☐ 19:1-43	☐ 20:1—21:22	☐ 22:1-51	☐ 23:1-39	☐ 24:1-25	☐ 1 Kings 1:1-19	☐ 1:20-53
41	☐ 2:1-46	☐ 3:1-28	☐ 4:1-34	☐ 5:1—6:38	☐ 7:1-22	☐ 7:23-51	☐ 8:1-36
42	☐ 8:37-66	☐ 9:1-28	☐ 10:1-29	☐ 11:1-43	☐ 12:1-33	☐ 13:1-34	☐ 14:1-31
43	☐ 15:1-34	☐ 16:1—17:24	☐ 18:1-46	☐ 19:1-21	☐ 20:1-43	☐ 21:1—22:53	☐ 2 Kings 1:1-18
44	☐ 2:1—3:27	☐ 4:1-44	☐ 5:1—6:33	☐ 7:1-20	☐ 8:1-29	☐ 9:1-37	☐ 10:1-36
45	☐ 11:1—12:21	☐ 13:1—14:29	☐ 15:1-38	☐ 16:1-20	☐ 17:1-41	☐ 18:1-37	☐ 19:1-37
46	☐ 20:1—21:26	☐ 22:1-20	☐ 23:1-37	☐ 24:1—25:30	☐ 1 Chron 1:1-54	☐ 2:1—3:24	☐ 4:1—5:26
47	☐ 6:1-81	☐ 7:1-40	☐ 8:1-40	☐ 9:1-44	☐ 10:1—11:47	☐ 12:1-40	☐ 13:1—14:17
48	☐ 15:1—16:43	☐ 17:1-27	☐ 18:1—19:19	☐ 20:1—21:30	☐ 22:1—23:32	☐ 24:1—25:31	☐ 26:1-32
49	☐ 27:1-34	☐ 28:1—29:30	☐ 2 Chron 1:1-17	☐ 2:1—3:17	☐ 4:1—5:14	☐ 6:1-42	☐ 7:1—8:18
50	☐ 9:1—10:19	☐ 11:1—12:16	☐ 13:1—15:19	☐ 16:1—17:19	☐ 18:1—19:11	☐ 20:1-37	☐ 21:1—22:12
51	☐ 23:1—24:27	☐ 25:1—26:23	☐ 27:1—28:27	☐ 29:1-36	☐ 30:1—31:21	☐ 32:1-33	☐ 33:1—34:33
52	☐ 35:1—36:23	☐ Ezra 1:1-11	☐ 2:1-70	☐ 3:1—4:24	☐ 5:1—6:22	☐ 7:1-28	☐ 8:1-36

Wk.	Lord's Day	Monday	Tuesday	Wednesday	Thursday	Friday	Saturday
53	☐ 9:1—10:44	☐ Neh 1:1-11	☐ 2:1—3:32	☐ 4:1—5:19	☐ 6:1-19	☐ 7:1-73	☐ 8:1-18
54	☐ 9:1-20	☐ 9:21-38	☐ 10:1—11:36	☐ 12:1-47	☐ 13:1-31	☐ Esth 1:1-22	☐ 2:1—3:15
55	☐ 4:1—5:14	☐ 6:1—7:10	☐ 8:1-17	☐ 9:1—10:3	☐ Job 1:1-22	☐ 2:1—3:26	☐ 4:1—5:27
56	☐ 6:1—7:21	☐ 8:1—9:35	☐ 10:1—11:20	☐ 12:1—13:28	☐ 14:1—15:35	☐ 16:1—17:16	☐ 18:1—19:29
57	☐ 20:1—21:34	☐ 22:1—23:17	☐ 24:1—25:6	☐ 26:1—27:23	☐ 28:1—29:25	☐ 30:1—31:40	☐ 32:1—33:33
58	☐ 34:1—35:16	☐ 36:1-33	☐ 37:1-24	☐ 38:1-41	☐ 39:1-30	☐ 40:1-24	☐ 41:1-34
59	☐ 42:1-17	☐ Psa 1:1-6	☐ 2:1—3:8	☐ 4:1—6:10	☐ 7:1—8:9	☐ 9:1—10:18	☐ 11:1—15:5
60	☐ 16:1—17:15	☐ 18:1-50	☐ 19:1—21:13	☐ 22:1-31	☐ 23:1—24:10	☐ 25:1—27:14	☐ 28:1—30:12
61	☐ 31:1—32:11	☐ 33:1—34:22	☐ 35:1—36:12	☐ 37:1-40	☐ 38:1—39:13	☐ 40:1—41:13	☐ 42:1—43:5
62	☐ 44:1-26	☐ 45:1-17	☐ 46:1—48:14	☐ 49:1—50:23	☐ 51:1—52:9	☐ 53:1—55:23	☐ 56:1—58:11
63	☐ 59:1—61:8	☐ 62:1—64:10	☐ 65:1—67:7	☐ 68:1-35	☐ 69:1—70:5	☐ 71:1—72:20	☐ 73:1—74:23
64	☐ 75:1—77:20	☐ 78:1-72	☐ 79:1—81:16	☐ 82:1—84:12	☐ 85:1—87:7	☐ 88:1—89:52	☐ 90:1—91:16
65	☐ 92:1—94:23	☐ 95:1—97:12	☐ 98:1—101:8	☐ 102:1—103:22	☐ 104:1—105:45	☐ 106:1-48	☐ 107:1-43
66	☐ 108:1—109:31	☐ 110:1—112:10	☐ 113:1—115:18	☐ 116:1—118:29	☐ 119:1-32	☐ 119:33-72	☐ 119:73-120
67	☐ 119:121-176	☐ 120:1—124:8	☐ 125:1—128:6	☐ 129:1—132:18	☐ 133:1—135:21	☐ 136:1—138:8	☐ 139:1—140:13
68	☐ 141:1—144:15	☐ 145:1—147:20	☐ 148:1—150:6	☐ Prov 1:1-33	☐ 2:1—3:35	☐ 4:1—5:23	☐ 6:1-35
69	☐ 7:1—8:36	☐ 9:1—10:32	☐ 11:1—12:28	☐ 13:1—14:35	☐ 15:1-33	☐ 16:1-33	☐ 17:1-28
70	☐ 18:1-24	☐ 19:1—20:30	☐ 21:1—22:29	☐ 23:1—35	☐ 24:1—25:28	☐ 26:1—27:27	☐ 28:1—29:27
71	☐ 30:1-33	☐ 31:1-31	☐ Eccl 1:1-18	☐ 2:1—3:22	☐ 4:1—5:20	☐ 6:1—7:29	☐ 8:1—9:18
72	☐ 10:1—11:10	☐ 12:1-14	☐ S.S 1:1-8	☐ 1:9-17	☐ 2:1-17	☐ 3:1-11	☐ 4:1-8
73	☐ 4:9-16	☐ 5:1-16	☐ 6:1-13	☐ 7:1-13	☐ 8:1-14	☐ Isa 1:1-11	☐ 1:12-31
74	☐ 2:1-22	☐ 3:1-26	☐ 4:1-6	☐ 5:1-30	☐ 6:1-13	☐ 7:1-25	☐ 8:1-22
75	☐ 9:1-21	☐ 10:1-34	☐ 11:1—12:6	☐ 13:1-22	☐ 14:1-14	☐ 14:15-32	☐ 15:1—16:14
76	☐ 17:1—18:7	☐ 19:1-25	☐ 20:1—21:17	☐ 22:1-25	☐ 23:1-18	☐ 24:1-23	☐ 25:1-12
77	☐ 26:1—:21	☐ 27:1-13	☐ 28:1-29	☐ 29:1-24	☐ 30:1-33	☐ 31:1—32:20	☐ 33:1-24
78	☐ 34:1-17	☐ 35:1-10	☐ 36:1-22	☐ 37:1-38	☐ 38:1—39:8	☐ 40:1-31	☐ 41:1-29

Reading Schedule for the Recovery Version of the Old Testament with Footnotes

Wk.	Lord's Day	Monday	Tuesday	Wednesday	Thursday	Friday	Saturday
79	☐ 42:1-25	☐ 43:1-28	☐ 44:1-28	☐ 45:1-25	☐ 46:1-13	☐ 47:1-15	☐ 48:1-22
80	☐ 49:1-13	☐ 49:14-26	☐ 50:1—51:23	☐ 52:1-15	☐ 53:1-12	☐ 54:1-17	☐ 55:1-13
81	☐ 56:1-12	☐ 57:1-21	☐ 58:1-14	☐ 59:1-21	☐ 60:1-22	☐ 61:1-11	☐ 62:1-12
82	☐ 63:1-19	☐ 64:1-12	☐ 65:1-25	☐ 66:1-24	☐ Jer 1:1-19	☐ 2:1-19	☐ 2:20-37
83	☐ 3:1-25	☐ 4:1-31	☐ 5:1-31	☐ 6:1-30	☐ 7:1-34	☐ 8:1-22	☐ 9:1-26
84	☐ 10:1-25	☐ 11:1—12:17	☐ 13:1-27	☐ 14:1-22	☐ 15:1-21	☐ 16:1—17:27	☐ 18:1-23
85	☐ 19:1—20:18	☐ 21:1—22:30	☐ 23:1-40	☐ 24:1—25:38	☐ 26:1—27:22	☐ 28:1—29:32	☐ 30:1-24
86	☐ 31:1-23	☐ 31:24-40	☐ 32:1-44	☐ 33:1-26	☐ 34:1-22	☐ 35:1-19	☐ 36:1-32
87	☐ 37:1-21	☐ 38:1-28	☐ 39:1—40:16	☐ 41:1—42:22	☐ 43:1—44:30	☐ 45:1—46:28	☐ 47:1—48:16
88	☐ 48:17-47	☐ 49:1-22	☐ 49:23-39	☐ 50:1-27	☐ 50:28-46	☐ 51:1-27	☐ 51:28-64
89	☐ 52:1-34	☐ Lam 1:1-22	☐ 2:1-22	☐ 3:1-39	☐ 3:40-66	☐ 4:1-22	☐ 5:1-22
90	☐ Ezek 1:1-14	☐ 1:15-28	☐ 2:1—3:27	☐ 4:1—5:17	☐ 6:1—7:27	☐ 8:1—9:11	☐ 10:1—11:25
91	☐ 12:1—13:23	☐ 14:1—15:8	☐ 16:1-63	☐ 17:1—18:32	☐ 19:1-14	☐ 20:1-49	☐ 21:1-32
92	☐ 22:1-31	☐ 23:1-49	☐ 24:1-27	☐ 25:1—26:21	☐ 27:1-36	☐ 28:1-26	☐ 29:1—30:26
93	☐ 31:1—32:32	☐ 33:1-33	☐ 34:1-31	☐ 35:1—36:21	☐ 36:22-38	☐ 37:1-28	☐ 38:1—39:29
94	☐ 40:1-27	☐ 40:28-49	☐ 41:1-26	☐ 42:1—43:27	☐ 44:1-31	☐ 45:1-25	☐ 46:1-24
95	☐ 47:1-23	☐ 48:1-35	☐ Dan 1:1-21	☐ 2:1-30	☐ 2:31-49	☐ 3:1-30	☐ 4:1-37
96	☐ 5:1-31	☐ 6:1-28	☐ 7:1-12	☐ 7:13-28	☐ 8:1-27	☐ 9:1-27	☐ 10:1-21
97	☐ 11:1-22	☐ 11:23-45	☐ 12:1-13	☐ Hosea 1:1-11	☐ 2:1-23	☐ 3:1—4:19	☐ 5:1-15
98	☐ 6:1-11	☐ 7:1-16	☐ 8:1-14	☐ 9:1-17	☐ 10:1-15	☐ 11:1-12	☐ 12:1-14
99	☐ 13:1—14:9	☐ Joel 1:1-20	☐ 2:1-16	☐ 2:17-32	☐ 3:1-21	☐ Amos 1:1-15	☐ 2:1-16
100	☐ 3:1-15	☐ 4:1—5:27	☐ 6:1—7:17	☐ 8:1—9:15	☐ Obad 1-21	☐ Jonah 1:1-17	☐ 2:1—4:11
101	☐ Micah 1:1-16	☐ 2:1—3:12	☐ 4:1—5:15	☐ 6:1—7:20	☐ Nahum 1:1-15	☐ 2:1—3:19	☐ Hab 1:1-17
102	☐ 2:1-20	☐ 3:1-19	☐ Zeph 1:1-18	☐ 2:1-15	☐ 3:1-20	☐ Hag 1:1-15	☐ 2:1-23
103	☐ Zech 1:1-21	☐ 2:1-13	☐ 3:1-10	☐ 4:1-14	☐ 5:1—6:15	☐ 7:1—8:23	☐ 9:1-17
104	☐ 10:1—11:17	☐ 12:1—13:9	☐ 14:1-21	☐ Mal 1:1-14	☐ 2:1-17	☐ 3:1-18	☐ 4:1-6

Reading Schedule for the Recovery Version of the New Testament with Footnotes

Wk.	Lord's Day	Monday	Tuesday	Wednesday	Thursday	Friday	Saturday
1	☐ Matt 1:1-2	☐ 1:3-7	☐ 1:8-17	☐ 1:18-25	☐ 2:1-23	☐ 3:1-6	☐ 3:7-17
2	☐ 4:1-11	☐ 4:12-25	☐ 5:1-4	☐ 5:5-12	☐ 5:13-20	☐ 5:21-26	☐ 5:27-48
3	☐ 6:1-8	☐ 6:9-18	☐ 6:19-34	☐ 7:1-12	☐ 7:13-29	☐ 8:1-13	☐ 8:14-22
4	☐ 8:23-34	☐ 9:1-13	☐ 9:14-17	☐ 9:18-34	☐ 9:35—10:5	☐ 10:6-25	☐ 10:26-42
5	☐ 11:1-15	☐ 11:16-30	☐ 12:1-14	☐ 12:15-32	☐ 12:33-42	☐ 12:43—13:2	☐ 13:3-12
6	☐ 13:13-30	☐ 13:31-43	☐ 13:44-58	☐ 14:1-13	☐ 14:14-21	☐ 14:22-36	☐ 15:1-20
7	☐ 15:21-31	☐ 15:32-39	☐ 16:1-12	☐ 16:13-20	☐ 16:21-28	☐ 17:1-13	☐ 17:14-27
8	☐ 18:1-14	☐ 18:15-22	☐ 18:23-35	☐ 19:1-15	☐ 19:16-30	☐ 20:1-16	☐ 20:17-34
9	☐ 21:1-11	☐ 21:12-22	☐ 21:23-32	☐ 21:33-46	☐ 22:1-22	☐ 22:23-33	☐ 22:34-46
10	☐ 23:1-12	☐ 23:13-39	☐ 24:1-14	☐ 24:15-31	☐ 24:32-51	☐ 25:1-13	☐ 25:14-30
11	☐ 25:31-46	☐ 26:1-16	☐ 26:17-35	☐ 26:36-46	☐ 26:47-64	☐ 26:65-75	☐ 27:1-26
12	☐ 27:27-44	☐ 27:45-56	☐ 27:57—28:15	☐ 28:16-20	☐ Mark 1:1	☐ 1:2-6	☐ 1:7-13
13	☐ 1:14-28	☐ 1:29-45	☐ 2:1-12	☐ 2:13-28	☐ 3:1-19	☐ 3:20-35	☐ 4:1-25
14	☐ 4:26-41	☐ 5:1-20	☐ 5:21-43	☐ 6:1-29	☐ 6:30-56	☐ 7:1-23	☐ 7:24-37
15	☐ 8:1-26	☐ 8:27—9:1	☐ 9:2-29	☐ 9:30-50	☐ 10:1-16	☐ 10:17-34	☐ 10:35-52
16	☐ 11:1-16	☐ 11:17-33	☐ 12:1-27	☐ 12:28-44	☐ 13:1-13	☐ 13:14-37	☐ 14:1-26
17	☐ 14:27-52	☐ 14:53-72	☐ 15:1-15	☐ 15:16-47	☐ 16:1-8	☐ 16:9-20	☐ Luke 1:1-4
18	☐ 1:5-25	☐ 1:26-46	☐ 1:47-56	☐ 1:57-80	☐ 2:1-8	☐ 2:9-20	☐ 2:21-39
19	☐ 2:40-52	☐ 3:1-20	☐ 3:21-38	☐ 4:1-13	☐ 4:14-30	☐ 4:31-44	☐ 5:1-26
20	☐ 5:27—6:16	☐ 6:17-38	☐ 6:39-49	☐ 7:1-17	☐ 7:18-23	☐ 7:24-35	☐ 7:36-50
21	☐ 8:1-15	☐ 8:16-25	☐ 8:26-39	☐ 8:40-56	☐ 9:1-17	☐ 9:18-26	☐ 9:27-36
22	☐ 9:37-50	☐ 9:51-62	☐ 10:1-11	☐ 10:12-24	☐ 10:25-37	☐ 10:38-42	☐ 11:1-13
23	☐ 11:14-26	☐ 11:27-36	☐ 11:37-54	☐ 12:1-12	☐ 12:13-21	☐ 12:22-34	☐ 12:35-48
24	☐ 12:49-59	☐ 13:1-9	☐ 13:10-17	☐ 13:18-30	☐ 13:31—14:6	☐ 14:7-14	☐ 14:15-24
25	☐ 14:25-35	☐ 15:1-10	☐ 15:11-21	☐ 15:22-32	☐ 16:1-13	☐ 16:14-22	☐ 16:23-31
26	☐ 17:1-19	☐ 17:20-37	☐ 18:1-14	☐ 18:15-30	☐ 18:31-43	☐ 19:1-10	☐ 19:11-27

Reading Schedule for the Recovery Version of the New Testament with Footnotes

Wk.	Lord's Day	Monday	Tuesday	Wednesday	Thursday	Friday	Saturday
27	☐ Luke 19:28-48	☐ 20:1-19	☐ 20:20-38	☐ 20:39—21:4	☐ 21:5-27	☐ 21:28-38	☐ 22:1-20
28	☐ 22:21-38	☐ 22:39-54	☐ 22:55-71	☐ 23:1-43	☐ 23:44-56	☐ 24:1-12	☐ 24:13-35
29	☐ 24:36-53	☐ John 1:1-13	☐ 1:14-18	☐ 1:19-34	☐ 1:35-51	☐ 2:1-11	☐ 2:12-22
30	☐ 2:23—3:13	☐ 3:14-21	☐ 3:22-36	☐ 4:1-14	☐ 4:15-26	☐ 4:27-42	☐ 4:43-54
31	☐ 5:1-16	☐ 5:17-30	☐ 5:31-47	☐ 6:1-15	☐ 6:16-31	☐ 6:32-51	☐ 6:52-71
32	☐ 7:1-9	☐ 7:10-24	☐ 7:25-36	☐ 7:37-52	☐ 7:53—8:11	☐ 8:12-27	☐ 8:28-44
33	☐ 8:45-59	☐ 9:1-13	☐ 9:14-34	☐ 9:35—10:9	☐ 10:10-30	☐ 10:31—11:4	☐ 11:5-22
34	☐ 11:23-40	☐ 11:41-57	☐ 12:1-11	☐ 12:12-24	☐ 12:25-36	☐ 12:37-50	☐ 13:1-11
35	☐ 13:12-30	☐ 13:31-38	☐ 14:1-6	☐ 14:7-20	☐ 14:21-31	☐ 15:1-11	☐ 15:12-27
36	☐ 16:1-15	☐ 16:16-33	☐ 17:1-5	☐ 17:6-13	☐ 17:14-24	☐ 17:25—18:11	☐ 18:12-27
37	☐ 18:28-40	☐ 19:1-16	☐ 19:17-30	☐ 19:31-42	☐ 20:1-13	☐ 20:14-18	☐ 20:19-22
38	☐ 20:23-31	☐ 21:1-14	☐ 21:15-22	☐ 21:23-25	☐ Acts 1:1-8	☐ 1:9-14	☐ 1:15-26
39	☐ 2:1-13	☐ 2:14-21	☐ 2:22-36	☐ 2:37-41	☐ 2:42-47	☐ 3:1-18	☐ 3:19—4:22
40	☐ 4:23-37	☐ 5:1-16	☐ 5:17-32	☐ 5:33-42	☐ 6:1—7:1	☐ 7:2-29	☐ 7:30-60
41	☐ 8:1-13	☐ 8:14-25	☐ 8:26-40	☐ 9:1-19	☐ 9:20-43	☐ 10:1-16	☐ 10:17-33
42	☐ 10:34-48	☐ 11:1-18	☐ 11:19-30	☐ 12:1-25	☐ 13:1-12	☐ 13:13-43	☐ 13:44—14:5
43	☐ 14:6-28	☐ 15:1-12	☐ 15:13-34	☐ 15:35—16:5	☐ 16:6-18	☐ 16:19-40	☐ 17:1-18
44	☐ 17:19-34	☐ 18:1-17	☐ 18:18-28	☐ 19:1-20	☐ 19:21-41	☐ 20:1-12	☐ 20:13-38
45	☐ 21:1-14	☐ 21:15-26	☐ 21:27-40	☐ 22:1-21	☐ 22:22-29	☐ 22:30—23:11	☐ 23:12-15
46	☐ 23:16-30	☐ 23:31—24:21	☐ 24:22—25:5	☐ 25:6-27	☐ 26:1-13	☐ 26:14-32	☐ 27:1-26
47	☐ 27:27—28:10	☐ 28:11-22	☐ 28:23-31	☐ Rom 1:1-2	☐ 1:3-7	☐ 1:8-17	☐ 1:18-25
48	☐ 1:26—2:10	☐ 2:11-29	☐ 3:1-20	☐ 3:21-31	☐ 4:1-12	☐ 4:13-25	☐ 5:1-11
49	☐ 5:12-17	☐ 5:18—6:5	☐ 6:6-11	☐ 6:12-23	☐ 7:1-12	☐ 7:13-25	☐ 8:1-2
50	☐ 8:3-6	☐ 8:7-13	☐ 8:14-25	☐ 8:26-39	☐ 9:1-18	☐ 9:19—10:3	☐ 10:4-15
51	☐ 10:16—11:10	☐ 11:11-22	☐ 11:23-36	☐ 12:1-3	☐ 12:4-21	☐ 13:1-14	☐ 14:1-12
52	☐ 14:13-23	☐ 15:1-13	☐ 15:14-33	☐ 16:1-5	☐ 16:6-24	☐ 16:25-27	☐ 1 Cor 1:1-4

Reading Schedule for the Recovery Version of the New Testament with Footnotes

Wk.	Lord's Day	Monday	Tuesday	Wednesday	Thursday	Friday	Saturday
53	☐ 1 Cor 1:5-9	☐ 1:10-17	☐ 1:18-31	☐ 2:1-5	☐ 2:6-10	☐ 2:11-16	☐ 3:1-9
54	☐ 3:10-13	☐ 3:14-23	☐ 4:1-9	☐ 4:10-21	☐ 5:1-13	☐ 6:1-11	☐ 6:12-20
55	☐ 7:1-16	☐ 7:17-24	☐ 7:25-40	☐ 8:1-13	☐ 9:1-15	☐ 9:16-27	☐ 10:1-4
56	☐ 10:5-13	☐ 10:14-33	☐ 11:1-6	☐ 11:7-16	☐ 11:17-26	☐ 11:27-34	☐ 12:1-11
57	☐ 12:12-22	☐ 12:23-31	☐ 13:1-13	☐ 14:1-12	☐ 14:13-25	☐ 14:26-33	☐ 14:34-40
58	☐ 15:1-19	☐ 15:20-28	☐ 15:29-34	☐ 15:35-49	☐ 15:50-58	☐ 16:1-9	☐ 16:10-24
59	☐ 2 Cor 1:1-4	☐ 1:5-14	☐ 1:15-22	☐ 1:23—2:11	☐ 2:12-17	☐ 3:1-6	☐ 3:7-11
60	☐ 3:12-18	☐ 4:1-6	☐ 4:7-12	☐ 4:13-18	☐ 5:1-8	☐ 5:9-15	☐ 5:16-21
61	☐ 6:1-13	☐ 6:14—7:4	☐ 7:5-16	☐ 8:1-15	☐ 8:16-24	☐ 9:1-15	☐ 10:1-6
62	☐ 10:7-18	☐ 11:1-15	☐ 11:16-33	☐ 12:1-10	☐ 12:11-21	☐ 13:1-10	☐ 13:11-14
63	☐ Gal 1:1-5	☐ 1:6-14	☐ 1:15-24	☐ 2:1-13	☐ 2:14-21	☐ 3:1-4	☐ 3:5-14
64	☐ 3:15-22	☐ 3:23-29	☐ 4:1-7	☐ 4:8-20	☐ 4:21-31	☐ 5:1-12	☐ 5:13-21
65	☐ 5:22-26	☐ 6:1-10	☐ 6:11-15	☐ 6:16-18	☐ Eph 1:1-3	☐ 1:4-6	☐ 1:7-10
66	☐ 1:11-14	☐ 1:15-18	☐ 1:19-23	☐ 2:1-5	☐ 2:6-10	☐ 2:11-14	☐ 2:15-18
67	☐ 2:19-22	☐ 3:1-7	☐ 3:8-13	☐ 3:14-18	☐ 3:19-21	☐ 4:1-4	☐ 4:5-10
68	☐ 4:11-16	☐ 4:17-24	☐ 4:25-32	☐ 5:1-10	☐ 5:11-21	☐ 5:22-26	☐ 5:27-33
69	☐ 6:1-9	☐ 6:10-14	☐ 6:15-18	☐ 6:19-24	☐ Phil 1:1-7	☐ 1:8-18	☐ 1:19-26
70	☐ 1:27—2:4	☐ 2:5-11	☐ 2:12-16	☐ 2:17-30	☐ 3:1-6	☐ 3:7-11	☐ 3:12-16
71	☐ 3:17-21	☐ 4:1-9	☐ 4:10-23	☐ Col 1:1-8	☐ 1:9-13	☐ 1:14-23	☐ 1:24-29
72	☐ 2:1-7	☐ 2:8-15	☐ 2:16-23	☐ 3:1-4	☐ 3:5-15	☐ 3:16-25	☐ 4:1-18
73	☐ 1 Thes 1:1-3	☐ 1:4-10	☐ 2:1-12	☐ 2:13—3:5	☐ 3:6-13	☐ 4:1-10	☐ 4:11—5:11
74	☐ 5:12-28	☐ 2 Thes 1:1-12	☐ 2:1-17	☐ 3:1-18	☐ 1 Tim 1:1-2	☐ 1:3-4	☐ 1:5-14
75	☐ 1:15-20	☐ 2:1-7	☐ 2:8-15	☐ 3:1-13	☐ 3:14—4:5	☐ 4:6-16	☐ 5:1-25
76	☐ 6:1-10	☐ 6:11-21	☐ 2 Tim 1:1-10	☐ 1:11-18	☐ 2:1-15	☐ 2:16-26	☐ 3:1-13
77	☐ 3:14—4:8	☐ 4:9-22	☐ Titus 1:1-4	☐ 1:5-16	☐ 2:1-15	☐ 3:1-8	☐ 3:9-15
78	☐ Philem 1:1-11	☐ 1:12-25	☐ Heb 1:1-2	☐ 1:3-5	☐ 1:6-14	☐ 2:1-9	☐ 2:10-18

Reading Schedule for the Recovery Version of the New Testament with Footnotes

Wk.	Lord's Day	Monday	Tuesday	Wednesday	Thursday	Friday	Saturday
79	☐ Heb 3:1-6	☐ 3:7-19	☐ 4:1-9	☐ 4:10-13	☐ 4:14-16	☐ 5:1-10	☐ 5:11—6:3
80	☐ 6:4-8	☐ 6:9-20	☐ 7:1-10	☐ 7:11-28	☐ 8:1-6	☐ 8:7-13	☐ 9:1-4
81	☐ 9:5-14	☐ 9:15-28	☐ 10:1-18	☐ 10:19-28	☐ 10:29-39	☐ 11:1-6	☐ 11:7-19
82	☐ 11:20-31	☐ 11:32-40	☐ 12:1-2	☐ 12:3-13	☐ 12:14-17	☐ 12:18-26	☐ 12:27-29
83	☐ 13:1-7	☐ 13:8-12	☐ 13:13-15	☐ 13:16-25	☐ James 1:1-8	☐ 1:9-18	☐ 1:19-27
84	☐ 2:1-13	☐ 2:14-26	☐ 3:1-18	☐ 4:1-10	☐ 4:11-17	☐ 5:1-12	☐ 5:13-20
85	☐ 1 Pet 1:1-2	☐ 1:3-4	☐ 1:5	☐ 1:6-9	☐ 1:10-12	☐ 1:13-17	☐ 1:18-25
86	☐ 2:1-3	☐ 2:4-8	☐ 2:9-17	☐ 2:18-25	☐ 3:1-13	☐ 3:14-22	☐ 4:1-6
87	☐ 4:7-16	☐ 4:17-19	☐ 5:1-4	☐ 5:5-9	☐ 5:10-14	☐ 2 Pet 1:1-2	☐ 1:3-4
88	☐ 1:5-8	☐ 1:9-11	☐ 1:12-18	☐ 1:19-21	☐ 2:1-3	☐ 2:4-11	☐ 2:12-22
89	☐ 3:1-6	☐ 3:7-9	☐ 3:10-12	☐ 3:13-15	☐ 3:16	☐ 3:17-18	☐ 1 John 1:1-2
90	☐ 1:3-4	☐ 1:5	☐ 1:6	☐ 1:7	☐ 1:8-10	☐ 2:1-2	☐ 2:3-11
91	☐ 2:12-14	☐ 2:15-19	☐ 2:20-23	☐ 2:24-27	☐ 2:28-29	☐ 3:1-5	☐ 3:6-10
92	☐ 3:11-18	☐ 3:19-24	☐ 4:1-6	☐ 4:7-11	☐ 4:12-15	☐ 4:16—5:3	☐ 5:4-13
93	☐ 5:14-17	☐ 5:18-21	☐ 2 John 1:1-3	☐ 1:4-9	☐ 1:10-13	☐ 3 John 1:1-6	☐ 1:7-14
94	☐ Jude 1:1-4	☐ 1:5-10	☐ 1:11-19	☐ 1:20-25	☐ Rev 1:1-3	☐ 1:4-6	☐ 1:7-11
95	☐ 1:12-13	☐ 1:14-16	☐ 1:17-20	☐ 2:1-6	☐ 2:7	☐ 2:8-9	☐ 2:10-11
96	☐ 2:12-14	☐ 2:15-17	☐ 2:18-23	☐ 2:24-29	☐ 3:1-3	☐ 3:4-6	☐ 3:7-9
97	☐ 3:10-13	☐ 3:14-18	☐ 3:19-22	☐ 4:1-5	☐ 4:6-7	☐ 4:8-11	☐ 5:1-6
98	☐ 5:7-14	☐ 6:1-8	☐ 6:9-17	☐ 7:1-8	☐ 7:9-17	☐ 8:1-6	☐ 8:7-12
99	☐ 8:13—9:11	☐ 9:12-21	☐ 10:1-4	☐ 10:5-11	☐ 11:1-4	☐ 11:5-14	☐ 11:15-19
100	☐ 12:1-4	☐ 12:5-9	☐ 12:10-18	☐ 13:1-10	☐ 13:11-18	☐ 14:1-5	☐ 14:6-12
101	☐ 14:13-20	☐ 15:1-8	☐ 16:1-12	☐ 16:13-21	☐ 17:1-6	☐ 17:7-18	☐ 18:1-8
102	☐ 18:9—19:4	☐ 19:5-10	☐ 19:11-16	☐ 19:17-21	☐ 20:1-6	☐ 20:7-10	☐ 20:11-15
103	☐ 21:1	☐ 21:2	☐ 21:3-8	☐ 21:9-13	☐ 21:14-18	☐ 21:19-21	☐ 21:22-27
104	☐ 22:1	☐ 22:2	☐ 22:3-11	☐ 22:12-15	☐ 22:16-17	☐ 22:18-21	

Week 1 — Day 4   Today's verses

Lev. ...If anyone sins without intent, in any of
4:2-3 the things which Jehovah has commanded
not to be done, and does any one of them,
if the anointed priest sins so as to bring
guilt on the people, then let him present a
bull of the herd without blemish to Jehovah for a sin offering for his sin that he
committed.

Week 1 — Day 5   Today's verses

1 John But if we walk in the light as He is in
1:7 the light, we have fellowship with one
another, and the blood of Jesus His Son
cleanses us from every sin.

Week 1 — Day 6   Today's verses

1 John ...If anyone sins, we have an Advocate
2:1-2 with the Father, Jesus Christ the Righteous; and He Himself is the propitiation
for our sins, and not for ours only but also
for *those of* the whole world.

Week 1 — Day 1   Today's verses

1 John That which we have seen and heard we
1:3 report also to you that you also may have
fellowship with us, and indeed our fellowship is with the Father and with His
Son Jesus Christ.

Rev. And he showed me a river of water of life,
22:1 bright as crystal, proceeding out of the
throne of God and of the Lamb in the
middle of its street.

2 Cor. The grace of the Lord Jesus Christ and the
13:14 love of God and the fellowship of the
Holy Spirit be with you all.

Week 1 — Day 2   Today's verses

Acts And they continued steadfastly in the
2:42 teaching and the fellowship of the apostles, in the breaking of bread and the
prayers.

Week 1 — Day 3   Today's verses

Phil. If there is therefore any encouragement in
2:1 Christ, if any consolation of love, if any
fellowship of spirit, if any tenderheartedness and compassions.

Week 2 — Day 1   Today's verses

1 John 1:4 — And these things we write that our joy may be made full.

3:24 — And he who keeps His commandments abides in Him, and He in him. And in this we know that He abides in us, by the Spirit whom He gave to us.

2 Cor. 13:14 — The grace of the Lord Jesus Christ and the love of God and the fellowship of the Holy Spirit be with you all.

Date

Week 2 — Day 2   Today's verses

1 John 1:2-3 — (And the life was manifested, and we have seen and testify and report to you the eternal life, which was with the Father and was manifested to us); that which we have seen and heard we report also to you that you also may have fellowship with us, and indeed our fellowship is with the Father and with His Son Jesus Christ.

4:10 — Herein is love, not that we have loved God but that He loved us and sent His Son as a propitiation for our sins.

Date

Week 2 — Day 3   Today's verses

1 John 5:11-12 — And this is the testimony, that God gave to us eternal life and this life is in His Son. He who has the Son has the life; he who does not have the Son of God does not have the life.

3:14 — We know that we have passed out of death into life because we love the brothers. He who does not love abides in death.

2:1-2 — My little children, these things I write to you that you may not sin. And if anyone sins, we have an Advocate with the Father, Jesus Christ the Righteous; and He Himself is the propitiation for our sins…

Date

Week 2 — Day 4   Today's verses

1 John 2:27 — And as for you, the anointing which you have received from Him abides in you, and you have no need that anyone teach you; but as His anointing teaches you concerning all things and is not a lie, and even as it has taught you, abide in Him.

4:13-14 — In this we know that we abide in Him and He in us, that He has given to us of His Spirit. And we have beheld and testify that the Father has sent the Son as the Savior of the world.

John 7:39 — But this He said concerning the Spirit, whom those who believed into Him were about to receive; for the Spirit was not yet, because Jesus had not yet been glorified.

Date

Week 2 — Day 5   Today's verses

1 John 2:27 — And as for you, the anointing which you have received from Him abides in you, and you have no need that anyone teach you; but as His anointing teaches you concerning all things and is true and is not a lie, and even as it has taught you, abide in Him.

4:15-16 — Whoever confesses that Jesus is the Son of God, God abides in him and he in God. And we know and have believed the love which God has in us. God is love, and he who abides in love abides in God and God abides in him.

Date

Week 2 — Day 6   Today's verses

Job 42:5 — I had heard of You by the hearing of the ear, / But now my eye has seen You.

3 John 11 — …He who does good is of God; he who does evil has not seen God.

1 John 3:20-21 — Because if our heart blames us, it is because God is greater than our heart and knows all things. Beloved, if our heart does not blame us, we have boldness toward God.

Date

Week 3 — Day 4 — Today's verses

1 John 1:1-3 — That which was from the beginning, which we have heard, which we have seen with our eyes, which we beheld and our hands handled, concerning the Word of life (and the life was manifested, and we have seen and testify and report to you the eternal life, which was with the Father and was manifested to us); that which we have seen and heard we report also to you that you also may have fellowship with us, and indeed our fellowship is with the Father and with His Son Jesus Christ.

John 1:1-2 — In the beginning was the Word, and the Word was with God, and the Word was God. He was in the beginning with God.

Date _____

Week 3 — Day 1 — Today's verses

1 John 1:1 — That which was from the beginning, which we have heard, which we have seen with our eyes, which we beheld and our hands handled, concerning the Word of life.

Date _____

Week 3 — Day 5 — Today's verses

1 Tim. 6:12 — Fight the good fight of the faith; lay hold on the eternal life, to which you were called and have confessed the good confession before many witnesses.

Matt. 19:29 — And everyone who has left houses or brothers or sisters or father or mother or children or fields for My name's sake shall receive a hundred times as much and shall inherit eternal life.

Date _____

Week 3 — Day 2 — Today's verses

1 Tim. 6:19 — Laying away for themselves a good foundation as a treasure for the future, that they may lay hold on that which is really life.

Date _____

Week 3 — Day 6 — Today's verses

John 4:24 — God is Spirit, and those who worship Him must worship in spirit and truthfulness.

1 John 4:16 — ...God is love, and he who abides in love abides in God and God abides in him.

1:5 — And this is the message which we have heard from Him and announce to you, that God is light and in Him is no darkness at all.

Date _____

Week 3 — Day 3 — Today's verses

Eph. 4:18 — Being darkened in their understanding, alienated from the life of God...

Rev. 22:1-2 — And he showed me a river of water of life, bright as crystal, proceeding out of the throne of God and of the Lamb in the middle of its street. And on this side and on that side of the river was the tree of life, producing twelve fruits, yielding its fruit each month; and the leaves of the tree are for the healing of the nations.

Date _____

Week 4 — Day 4   Today's verses

1 John 3:1 Behold what manner of love the Father has given to us, that we should be called children of God....

1 John 4:7 Beloved, let us love one another, because love is of God, and everyone who loves has been begotten of God and knows God.

Phil. 2:15 That you may be blameless and guileless, children of God without blemish in the midst of a crooked and perverted generation, among whom you shine as luminaries in the world.

Date

Week 4 — Day 5   Today's verses

1 John 2:29—3:1 If you know that He is righteous, you know that everyone who practices righteousness also has been begotten of Him. Behold what manner of love the Father has given to us, that we should be called children of God; and we are....

Rom. 8:16 The Spirit Himself witnesses with our spirit that we are children of God.

Gen. 1:26 ...God said, Let Us make man in Our image, according to Our likeness; and let them have dominion over the fish of the sea and over the birds of heaven and over the cattle and over all the earth and over every creeping thing that creeps upon the earth.

Date

Week 4 — Day 6   Today's verses

John 3:5 Jesus answered....Unless one is born of water and the Spirit, he cannot enter into the kingdom of God.

1 John 3:2 Beloved, now we are children of God, and it has not yet been manifested what we will be. We know that if He is manifested, we will be like Him because we will see Him even as He is.

Rom. 8:29 Because those whom He foreknew, He also predestinated to be conformed to the image of His Son, that He might be the Firstborn among many brothers.

Date

Week 4 — Day 1   Today's verses

John 1:12-13 But as many as received Him, to them He gave the authority to become children of God, to those who believe into His name, who were begotten not of blood, nor of the will of the flesh, nor of the will of man, but of God.

1 John 5:1 Everyone who believes that Jesus is the Christ has been begotten of God, and everyone who loves Him who has begotten him also who has been begotten of Him.

Date

Week 4 — Day 2   Today's verses

2 Cor. 5:17 So then if anyone is in Christ, *he is a* new creation. The old things have passed away; behold, they have become new.

Col. 3:10 And have put on the new man, which is being renewed unto full knowledge according to the image of Him who created him.

John 5:24 Truly, truly, I say to you, He who hears My word and believes Him who sent Me has eternal life, and does not come into judgment but has passed out of death into life.

Date

Week 4 — Day 3   Today's verses

John 3:6 That which is born of the flesh is flesh, and that which is born of the Spirit is spirit.

1 John 5:4 For everything that has been begotten of God overcomes the world; and this is the victory which has overcome the world—our faith.

1 Pet. 1:3 Blessed be the God and Father of our Lord Jesus Christ, who according to His great mercy has regenerated us unto a living hope through the resurrection of Jesus Christ from the dead.

Date

Week 5 — Day 4   **Today's verses**

Heb. …We who have fled for refuge to lay hold
6:18-20 of the hope set before *us*, which we have
as an anchor of the soul, both secure and
firm and which enters within the veil,
where the Forerunner, Jesus, has entered
for us.…

Matt. …"You shall love the Lord your God with
22:37 all your heart and with all your soul and
with all your mind."

_____
Date

Week 5 — Day 5   **Today's verses**

1 John If we confess our sins, He is faithful and
1:9 righteous to forgive us our sins and cleanse
us from all unrighteousness.

Heb. For the word of God is living and opera-
4:12 tive and sharper than any two-edged
sword, and piercing even to the dividing
of soul and spirit and of joints and
marrow, and able to discern the thoughts
and intentions of the heart.

_____
Date

Week 5 — Day 6   **Today's verses**

1 Pet. As newborn babes, long for the guileless
2:2 milk of the word in order that by it you
may grow unto salvation.

_____
Date

Week 5 — Day 1   **Today's verses**

John Jesus answered and said to him,.…Unless
3:3 one is born anew, he cannot see the kingdom of God.

6 That which is born of the flesh is flesh, and
that which is born of the Spirit is spirit.

Mark And He said, So is the kingdom of God: as
4:26-27 if a man cast seed on the earth, and sleeps
and rises night and day, and the seed
sprouts and lengthens.…

_____
Date

Week 5 — Day 2   **Today's verses**

1 John For everything that has been begotten of
5:4 God overcomes the world; and this is the
victory which has overcome the world—
our faith.

5:18-19 We know that everyone who is begotten
of God does not sin, but he who has been
begotten of God keeps himself, and the
evil one does not touch him. We know
that we are of God, and the whole world
lies in the evil one.

_____
Date

Week 5 — Day 3   **Today's verses**

1 John And we know that the Son of God has
5:20-21 come and has given us an understanding
that we might know Him who is true; and
we are in Him who is true, in His Son
Jesus Christ. This is the true God and eternal life. Little children, guard yourselves
from idols.

_____
Date

Week 6 — Day 1   Today's verses

1 John 1:5, 7   ...God is light and in Him is no darkness at all. ...But if we walk in the light as He is in the light, we have fellowship with one another, and the blood of Jesus His Son cleanses us from every sin.

2 Cor. 4:6   ...The God who said, Out of darkness light shall shine, is the One who shined in our hearts to illuminate the knowledge of the glory of God in the face of Jesus Christ.

_____
Date

Week 6 — Day 2   Today's verses

John 8:12   ...Jesus spoke to them, saying, I am the light of the world; he who follows Me shall by no means walk in darkness, but shall have the light of life.

32   And you shall know the truth, and the truth shall set you free.

Psa. 36:9   For with You is the fountain of life; / In Your light we see light.

_____
Date

Week 6 — Day 3   Today's verses

John 15:26   ...When the Comforter comes, whom I will send to you from the Father, the Spirit of reality, who proceeds from the Father, He will testify concerning Me.

16:13   But when He, the Spirit of reality, comes, He will guide you into all the reality; for He will not speak from Himself, but what He hears He will speak; and He will declare to you the things that are coming.

17:17   Sanctify them in the truth; Your word is truth.

_____
Date

Week 6 — Day 4   Today's verses

2 John 2   For the sake of the truth which abides in us and will be with us forever.

3 John 3-4   For I rejoiced greatly at the brothers' coming and testifying to your _steadfastness in the_ truth, even as you walk in truth. I have no greater joy than these things, that I hear that my children are walking in the truth.

_____
Date

Week 6 — Day 5   Today's verses

3 John 7-8   For on behalf of the Name they went out, taking nothing from the Gentiles. We therefore ought to support such ones that we may become fellow workers in the truth.

1 John 5:6   This is He who came through water and blood, Jesus Christ; not in the water only, but in the water and in the blood; and the Spirit is He who testifies, because the Spirit is the reality.

_____
Date

Week 6 — Day 6   Today's verses

2 John 1   The elder to the chosen lady and to her children, whom I love in truthfulness, and not only I but also all those who know the truth.

John 4:23-24   But an hour is coming, and it is now, when the true worshippers will worship the Father in spirit and truthfulness, for the Father also seeks such to worship Him. God is Spirit, and those who worship Him must worship in spirit and truthfulness.

_____
Date